XBOX
REVISITED

XBOX
REVISITED

A Game Plan for Corporate
and Civic Renewal

ROBBIE BACH

BROWN BOOKS
PUBLISHING GROUP

Xbox Revisited
A Game Plan for Corporate and Civic Renewal

Brown Books Publishing Group
16250 Knoll Trail Drive, Suite 205
Dallas, Texas 75248
www.BrownBooks.com
(972) 381-0009

A New Era in Publishing™

ISBN 978-1-61254-848-7
LCCN 2015941223

Printed in the United States
10 9 8 7 6 5 4 3 2 1

Author photo by Leslie Magid Higgins

For more information or to contact the author, please go to
www.RobbieBach.com
Twitter: @Robbie_Bach

For Pauline
My love, my friend, my soul mate

TABLE OF CONTENTS

A PERSONAL ACT II

I recently attended my twenty-fifth reunion at Stanford's Graduate School of Business—a traditional milestone to catch up with old friends, reconnect with others, and take stock of your professional development. Almost every conversation began with classmates trying to size up each other's accomplishments since our business school days. Stanford is a collegial place, but most of us are Type-A competitive personalities, and this mutual evaluation was just part of the reunion dance:

"So what are you doing now?"

"I retired from Microsoft after twenty-two years."

I'm sure my answer to this deceptively tame question left a hanging chad of doubt in many minds about my internal drive and motivation. Nobody retires at the age of forty-nine.

My decision to leave Microsoft in 2010, however, was not a retirement. It was a self-imposed period of reflection, a time to step back from the frenetic pace of my professional and personal lives to think deeply about how I wanted to have impact going forward. If my twenty-two years at Microsoft had impact in the business arena, how did I want my Act II to play out? How did I want to spend the next twenty-two years, more or less, to generate positive change beyond the corporate world? How could I take the lessons I'd learned from the challenges of building several successful businesses at Microsoft and apply them to broader civic and social issues? How could I have deep, lasting impact?

To explore the answers to these big life questions, I began writing. At first this was just an outlet—a way for me to express my frustrations, organize my thoughts, and evaluate opportunities for change. I reflected on the lasting value of my experiences as a leader at Microsoft, the transformative nature of my deep involvement with organizations like the Boys and Girls Clubs, and my belief in the power of sports to transcend differences. This combination of business experience, nonprofit commitment, and sports passion are unique traits that have shaped and formed my world view. When all of the evaluating was done, I found myself focusing on areas where I had real value to add—strategic thinking, organizational management, and driving change to address complex problems.

I went back to square one of the strategy process I had learned at Microsoft, in particular during my time creating and leading the Xbox business, and asked myself a few simple questions: "Could I create a practical strategy for bringing order to civic issues? Could my experiences in the world of video games translate to the tumultuous world of government and community organizations?" The irony implied in those questions was not lost on me, but I continued to write, and my transformation from business leader to aspiring citizen activist and self-described civic engineer was underway.

Xbox Revisited presents a common-sense, strategic framework for addressing complex problems. It can be used in personal, business, and civic contexts to plan new approaches and manage change effectively. It is also a case study that demonstrates how the Xbox team used early iterations of this strategic framework to build the business from a start-up to the leading video game company in the world. Most importantly, this book demonstrates how strategic business concepts can be applied to re-engineering our approach to civic matters. It is a call to action—a summons to each and every reader to recognize the challenges we face as a country and to demand that decisive action be taken. Ultimately, I want this book to ignite real conversation about the changes required to address the complex issues our nation faces.

Being patriotic and caring about our country may be somewhat old-fashioned, but I refuse to accept that the days when individuals could make a difference are over. I refuse to accept that we are powerless in our ability to change the direction of our country. I refuse to accept that civic issues are the province of think tanks, policy experts, and politicians.

I believe we can take on the challenges in our future, including highly complex ones that seem insurmountable or beyond our own abilities. To do that, we need two critical elements: a practical strategic framework that guides our actions and real leaders who can implement that strategy successfully. We need committed individuals who drive impact—change that has a deep, positive, social effect. I hope that *Xbox Revisited* can be a beacon of common-sense thinking that sets that type of change in motion.

THE DARKEST OF DAYS

I woke up in my hotel room in midtown Manhattan on September 11, 2001, ready for another day of grappling with the toughest challenge of my career at Microsoft. I had taken the red-eye from Seattle for a public relations tour to introduce journalists to the Xbox console, a critical step in our efforts to get Microsoft's entry into the video game business back on track.

Four months earlier, on May 16th, I had presided over the nightmarish Xbox launch event at E3, the gaming industry's largest and most important convention. The disaster had centered on the simplest of components: the on/off button. In theory, you press the button, the device turns on, and when you press it again, it turns off. Nothing fancy, complicated, or difficult involved; at least that is how it was supposed to work.

I remember standing at the podium at 8 a.m., ready to present Microsoft's game-changing console to a room full of hung-over E3 attendees. When I hit the Xbox on/off button, nothing happened—not a flicker, not a beep, not even a Microsoft blue screen. Just me and a silent, blank television. As Apollo 13 Commander Jim Lovell said, "Houston, we've had a problem here." Although our issues were not life threatening, there was no abort option. We still had to land Xbox on the moon, pick up the rocks, and bring them home. That moment was the beginning of a long, difficult mission.

Four months later, I was preparing for yet another day in the can-we-get-Xbox-launched challenge. September 11 actually began on the night of September 10 with a flight from Seattle to JFK airport in New York followed by a cab to the Marriot Marquis in Midtown. I went to sleep with no more cares in the world than my "rude Q&A" talking points for the difficult questions I would be asked on the tour. Oh . . . and we had just a few more manufacturing problems and the actual games might not be finished in time for launch. As Microsoft's Chief Xbox Officer (CXO), dealing with high-grade anxiety had become a way of life.

> Confused, I turned on the TV and realized that my press tour was cancelled, my trip was cut short, and America would never be the same.

I awoke a few hours later after a short nap, took a shower, and was putting on my suit of armor for some difficult meetings when the phone rang. The baritone voice on the other end of the line was unfamiliar, but then again, I'd never met the chief legal counsel from Edelman, our public relations firm. I could not imagine why the PR team had a lawyer calling me. Then, he mentioned an attack on the twin towers and said his office was across the street from my hotel if there was anything I needed. Confused, I turned on the TV and realized that my press tour was cancelled, my trip was cut short, and America would never be the same.

Early that same morning, my wife Pauline was out running with our yellow Labrador Charlie in the typical Seattle chill when a neighbor asked her if she'd seen the tragic news from New York. She quite literally sprinted home to see what had happened. For the next hour, she was frantic not knowing whether I was safe or not—all she knew was that I had flown into New York that morning. Just for that moment, while I was in New York cut off from communications and Pauline was in Seattle with no information, our minds shifted to all of the things we held dear in our lives. In moments of tragedy, fear, and the unknown, our priorities become crystal clear, and that revelation changes us in ways we don't immediately comprehend.

Getting out of New York after the attacks was nearly impossible. Airports were closed. Bridges were blocked. Trains weren't running. Finding a rental car took serious initiative and ingenuity. Luckily, those are common traits among Microsoft employees, and we reserved a Hertz rental for the next morning.

I shared the fifty-three-hour drive to Seattle in a Ford Taurus with Xbox PR manager James Bernard, Xbox events manager April McKee, and Craig Suhrbier, a Seattle friend who happened to be in New York. Although I wasn't thinking of it this way at the time, that trip across the country fundamentally changed my attitude toward the importance of civic issues and more particularly the direction of our country.

A CIVIC CALL TO ARMS

The terrorist attacks of 9/11 were a wakeup call, one that brought real perspective to my personal and professional challenges. Suddenly, the rattling noise troubling Xbox DVD drives became background clatter to the broader civic and social issues facing our country. In that moment, the national debate was dominated by questions of security, response, and yes, reprisal. A war had begun—one that has occupied our country for over a decade and changed our nation. The issues ran much deeper than our need to find Osama Bin Laden. Our country was facing a crisis of confidence and competence at every level across our civic landscape.

In the aftermath of the attacks, the United States changed in numerous ways, some for the better, but many for the worse. We certainly became more security conscious and less naïve about the world order and the inherent risks we face. We also demonstrated our ability to rally around those in need of help in times of national crisis and have continued to demonstrate that willingness through subsequent emergencies like Hurricane Katrina, the Sandy Hook murders, and the Boston Marathon bombing. These terrible events remind us we are all Americans, and, with rare exceptions, we act with solidarity of mind and unity of purpose.

Unfortunately, those underlying themes have been overwhelmed by a tremendous level of fragmentation and division. Our country has always had economic, social, and political divisions, but 9/11 was a giant leap, a jumping-off point. From one day to the next, the land of opportunity was fencing off its borders, profiling groups of citizens, and reducing civil liberties in ways unthinkable just a day earlier.

Several years later, a government predicated on the principles of compromise and common sense brought itself to a halt, literally and figuratively, through an inability to find obvious middle ground on the national budget. Special interest groups, always a problem in American politics, gained even more sway over our election process, and they utilized the threats of national security and economic Armageddon to argue for and against all kinds of extreme positions. Following the Great Recession of 2008, in a moment of total disgrace, our national credit rating was lowered, for the most part because our government was paralyzed and gridlocked.

These and other challenging issues involving our local, state, and federal institutions cannot be ignored. We the people must uphold the

American tradition of standing together during good times and bad. It's what we call "civic duty," and now is the time to rally to the cause.

If you look up "civics" in a dictionary, you will find a textbook definition that references the rights and duties of citizens and the responsibilities that come with citizenship. I would expand that classic definition to include responsibility for social, economic, and political matters. As citizens in a democracy, we have the task and privilege to engage with these issues in a constructive, productive manner. When we encounter important things that are "amiss," it is our civic duty to drive change.

And let us make no mistake that things are definitely amiss. As they say in *The Music Man*, "there is trouble in River City." While some of the challenges feel more immediate than others, America has deep, structural problems that must be addressed if we want to provide our children with a better future. We should not be confused: my generation—the generation in charge—is failing our children and our children's children. This is our country, and we have to take responsibility for its future. That means addressing the very problems we've created.

As I was mulling all of these issues, one of my old friends, Charles Roscovitch, sent me a letter that reflects so much of what I feel and believe about our civic health. Charles is a clear-thinking, common-sense kind of guy, and he describes the situation in a way that is objectively obvious and seemingly difficult for many civic leaders to accept:

December 1, 2012

Dear Robbie:
I hope that your retirement from Microsoft is treating you well and that your golf handicap is going down accordingly. I heard that Pauline has

kicked you out of the house into the cabana to do work—I'm sure you can play the role of Cabana Boy with great distinction!

On a more serious note, I was reflecting on the conversation we had about how you want to have impact in your "Act II" following Microsoft. Let me share some of my recent thinking on this particular topic—this won't be uplifting, but perhaps it will motivate you in the right way.

I've reached a very sad realization. After more than two hundred years of both tragedy and triumph, the country I love has arrived at a crossroads. While not the first such crossroads, we must acknowledge that the common, internal perception of our country as "the greatest nation on earth" is now contradicted by so many areas where we are falling short of that ambition. While we have much to be proud of, historians will clearly view the first decade of the new millennium as a time of civic challenge in the United States.

Our economy has barely survived the worst financial crisis in eighty years and is engaged in a long, difficult recovery. We have pursued two expensive wars with unclear goals and equally unclear results, draining our emotional and ethical reservoirs, to say nothing of our international credibility and financial capital. Our education system is no longer among the world's best and our national infrastructure is more fragile than at any time since World War II with many other areas in need of systematic upgrades and replacement.

A small percentage of business leaders, highlighted by but not limited to the financial services sector, have lost sight of their ethical and legal obligations, creating the perception that the broader business community is self-serving and soul-less. Our elected leaders have failed numerous times to construct and approve a budget, much less a broader strategic plan to drive sustainable activity. Instead they've just kicked the can down the road so that future generations will have to deal with an even bigger set of problems.

On a social level, the role of the family (of any form) as the core organizing unit has declined significantly creating a generation of children who lack a sound social foundation. We are steadily disenfranchising and indeed reducing the middle class, creating an economy and body politic divided between the "haves" and "have nots"—certainly not a recipe for a successful representative democracy. The extremism that now characterizes our social fabric has poisoned our ability to have useful discourse on real issues and find sensible, practical compromises.

As a result, public opinion of our business and government leaders has fallen to all-time lows, and that lack of respect makes effective leadership even more problematic. The result of all of these challenges (and many more) is gridlock on several levels, and we are paddling harder every year just to stay in the same place. Something must be done.

As you know, I am not a sociologist, political scientist, policy specialist, or government leader. Instead I claim the title of proud American citizen—a title I share with some three hundred million other individuals. I want to contribute something to change our trajectory as a country. In my mind, this requires a logical, common-sense approach to addressing the most important problems we face. It requires openness to change and a willingness to set aside personal, parochial interests to consider what is required for the good of the country as a whole. It demands that the sadly "silenced majority" that occupies the middle ground on most issues stands up and vocally asserts its power to drive real change. Courage, accountability, sacrifice, and commitment are the characteristics required to lead and drive this reformation.

I don't have all of the solutions, but I know our current leaders are failing the most basic tests of credibility. We need a national debate on what is truly important to us as a country, we need a strategic process at all levels of civic institutions to establish the important elements of achieving those goals, and we need leaders willing to make the difficult tradeoffs to ensure that the country turns in the right direction.

My apologies for the long treatise, but this is an important set of issues that anyone in a position of leadership should be addressing. I wanted you to know that I'm "all in" on this quest. . . . I hope you will join me.

Give my best to Pauline and the kids—and keep that dog of yours out of trouble.

Respectfully,
Charles

My friend professes to have little more than "dog sense," and yet what he says rings as true as a symphonic bell. We must ask ourselves, "What are our civic responsibilities and how are we going to fulfill them?" Unfortunately, many people don't see a path to influencing change or impacting the outcome. This hopelessness leads to apathy, and apathy is the beginning of the end.

Faced with overwhelming challenges at the advent of Xbox, I experienced this hopelessness in very real terms and even considered resigning from Microsoft. But during those darkest of days, with the Xbox launch in grave doubt, I learned that turning frustration and apathy into hope is strictly a function of practical thinking and proactive leadership. I believe we can apply the common-sense lessons learned during the Xbox project to these complex civic problems.

As citizens of our country, there is no national resignation letter. The time for delay and postponement is over. We need to recognize our problems, label them clearly for everyone to see, and develop an understandable strategy to tackle them. Neither Charles nor I think we can rely on those in Washington to begin the recovery process. That leaves the silent majority of Americans with the task of rolling up its sleeves, approaching problems analytically, and rallying fellow citizens to what is a noble and important cause. In fact, it is our civic duty.

This call to action has to be heard locally at Rotary Clubs, school boards, city councils, and other organizations. Nonprofits and businesses have to work together to craft private solutions to civic issues that have eluded our elected officials. Government leaders at all levels have to focus their priorities on what is right for citizens rather than what is right for their re-election campaigns. The right thing to do now, the common-sense thing, is to gear up for major, fundamental change.

All of which brings us to the central premise of *Xbox Revisited* and the questions I seek to answer: In a complex world whose evolution seems to be accelerating, how can we manage change effectively? Is there a strategic process to help us define clear initiatives that drive constructive change? Can the strategic framework developed in the Xbox business provide a pathway for tackling the difficult civic challenges we face across our country?

My answer is an emphatic yes. The most important lesson I learned at Microsoft was the critical need for common-sense strategies in response to complex challenges. Failures and missteps in the early development of Xbox led us to create a strategic framework that provided discipline and clarity for the Xbox team and paved the way to leadership in the gaming arena. I am convinced that what we learned in the rough and tumble video game entertainment business is translatable to the complex civic problems we face at all levels of our nation.

A FRAMEWORK FOR CHANGE

The strategy we developed for meeting our Xbox challenges is a practical, straightforward approach to tackling even the most difficult, intractable problems. I now call it the 3P Framework: Purpose, Principles, and Priorities. Communicate a clear purpose, commit to core principles, and establish a crisp set of priorities.

The 3P Framework is based on the premise that solving difficult problems requires a tremendous ability to simplify. Getting caught up in the complexity of a situation reduces our ability to grab the low-hanging fruit that creates momentum. When teams and individuals focus on purpose, principles, and priorities along with a short list of action items, they can tackle almost any type of problem—especially ones that feel the most intractable or complex.

> The 3P Framework is based on the premise that solving difficult problems requires a tremendous ability to simplify.

PURPOSE: THE SOUL OF THE MATTER

Every great, enduring strategy has a strong foundation—a touchstone that forms the core strategic direction for the group or organization. Purpose is a short, declarative statement that answers these questions: Why do we exist as an organization? What are we creating?

As the architectural basis for the strategy, an organization's purpose statement should require great thought and foresight. It has to be aspirational enough to stand the test of time yet realistic enough for people to believe it can be achieved. Although not immutable, purpose statements are meant to be long-lived directional beacons that change rarely and only then based on careful consideration.

PRINCIPLES: THE BELIEFS THAT MATTER

If purpose is the foundation for a strategy, principles are the frame of the house that create the shape and scope of the endeavor. Put another way, principles are the guard rails that ensure that organizations stay on course both strategically and morally, avoiding the inevitable distractions and marketplace noise that often mislead or confuse. Importantly, they enable employees to make real tradeoffs and decisions ensuring that the right tactics are pursued and prioritized correctly.

These statements (and there should be no more than five) reveal key beliefs about important strategy components such as customers, employees, and financial performance. They also codify certain elements of organizational culture that are important to the future success of the group. Principles are not specific programs or initiatives but rather are higher level concepts that endure for many years, in most cases changing only with a change in purpose.

PRIORITIES: THE ACTIONS THAT MATTER

With a solid foundation and support structure provided by purpose and principles, an organization can establish a set of priorities that lays out the rest of the strategy building. Priorities define the five (and no more than five) key initiatives and investments that will drive an organization over the next one to three years. These five priorities delineate the areas that must be resourced and managed successfully. Other tactical and operational programs will coexist or support these priorities, but any other major initiatives are either postponed or ignored altogether.

As a team moves into execution mode, more detailed plans are created to expand on the concepts in the 3P Framework to enable specific groups to operationalize the priorities that have been established.

Ultimately, they will write much more detailed plans to ensure that all of the specifics line up with the original concepts and approaches.

Once this strategic framework is in place, a leadership team creates matching measurable deliverables and objectives. At the end of each year or another appropriate period, the team evaluates progress in view of the priorities, makes adjustments, and creates the plan for the next period. In this way, the priorities of the strategic plan incorporate the flexibility necessary to stay current with changing conditions and the performance of the team. They also build the bridge from long-range strategic development to annual operational budgeting and planning.

In a nutshell, that is the 3P Framework. It's simple to understand, easy to communicate, and connected to the actual operations of an organization—common-sense characteristics particularly useful in tackling the types of complex challenges faced by businesses as well as civic and nonprofit organizations. None of this came to me in a flash of enlightenment. It's the reward of lessons learned from abject failures, gut-wrenching choices, and countless missteps that led eventually to gratifying successes in the Xbox business.

The 3P Framework was developed with a lot of input from my colleagues at Microsoft as we created the video game and entertainment technology that ultimately led a generation of gaming. In particular, I owe a huge debt of gratitude to my primary partner on the Xbox project, J Allard. I first encountered J at a meeting on Microsoft's Redwest campus in a famously odd part of Building C, complete with funky lights, bean bag furniture, and incoherent hallways. People often entered this area and couldn't find their way out.

At the time, J had hair colored in an electric shade of green or purple or whatever suited his mood that week. In most respects, he was the anti-Robbie, a trendy dresser at the cutting edge of design, entertainment, and everything else that defined the zeit-geist. He was a remarkable visionary. I, on the other hand, was the button-down business guy from the Midwest who cut his hair the same way he did in grade school and needed a fashion consultant from the PR team.

Our working relationship was rarely easy. We often disagreed, and I wanted to fire J several times. Of course, he wanted to quit just as many times, which created some equilibrium. Yet despite all our differences, we were united by a passion to win and a desire to build something great. Our brainstorming meetings yielded real results. If I was the business and organizational leader of Xbox, J was definitely the innovation and spiritual leader of the team, and J introduced or incubated much of what I have formalized in the 3P Framework. In our ten years on Xbox and other projects, J was the source of much inspiration and knowledge. We've not spent much time together since we left Microsoft, and I definitely miss his intellect, sense of humor, and irreverent spirit.

THE MAGIC OF 3 AND 5

The 3P Framework is predicated on the idea that great strategies focus on specific areas for action and investment, which brings us to Robbie's Rule of 3s and 5s. In most organizations, the challenge is not deciding which things should be on the laundry list of activities; usually the problem is determining what not to do and where to concentrate resources and energies.

The Rule of 3s states that if you want people to participate and truly internalize a strategy or a movement, you have to reduce the ideas to three simple points. Think of the power and clarity in our country's elemental three: "life, liberty, and the pursuit of happiness."

Christianity is based on the ultimate trio: the Father, the Son, and the Holy Spirit. Consider the enduring appeal of the trilogy in literature and the magic of the hat trick and the Triple Crown in sports. In my own experience, when I make presentations to large crowds or small groups, I find you get to present only three ideas, at most, if you want anyone to remember them.

The corollary to this triumvirate view of the world is that when you move from communication to action, people want to make things more complex. To be fair, setting goals and priorities often involves action on many fronts, and the list can become long and convoluted. Hence the Rule of 5s: any list of anything important that must be done ends after the fifth item. If you believe you must do item number seven, fine, but you need to replace one of the others in the top five.

In over twenty years of managing people, when I asked them to provide their objectives for the next six months, I usually got a long list of things they planned to accomplish. At their performance reviews, they inevitably reported, or tried not to report, that they didn't finish everything on their list. Certain items naturally fell off their plates, in large part because they couldn't focus on that many items at once. I learned to tell them they can only have five objectives because that is the most even the best people can handle. While frustrating for most Type-A personalities, this draconian approach reduced the intellectual baggage that collected around their work.

Resistance to the Rule of 3s and 5s is natural. Anyone who has a passion to accomplish great things imagines that a longer list of objectives signifies a larger vision or greater ambition. My experience tells me otherwise. Leaders have to require real, productive, and limited objectives from their teams. And team members have to understand that new, significant initiatives will be tackled, but only after the organization completes one or more of the top five priorities.

May 16, 2001 marked the shaky launch of Xbox, a revolutionary product marred by ineffective planning and execution. Four months later, September 11 seared our collective conscience, rearranged America's world view, altered our national psyche, and changed millions of lives. These two pivotal, dark days contributed something fundamental to my outlook on life. In the blink of an eye, they forced me to rethink my approach to problem solving, develop new approaches to leadership, and broaden my world view to include more than my little corner of the video game business.

The events of May 16 challenged me to accept that Xbox was in deep, deep trouble. We needed almost two years to transform the Xbox team and strategy, but on that day in May, I understood that serious action would be necessary to turn a fledgling start-up into a successful business. The tragedy of September 11 awoke me to the community realities around me. I needed almost ten years to understand the impact that day had on me and the rest of the nation, but the seed was deeply planted in my mind, waiting to be reborn. For me, these two dates go hand in hand in setting my agenda for the coming years. Indeed, the experience of reshaping the Xbox business was an essential element in developing a framework that I know can help us redefine our civic future.

2

IN THE BEGINNING

In over twenty years at Microsoft, I had the opportunity to manage and execute complex change in two important areas. The first was Microsoft Office, which applied new technology to old problems, literally reshaping the way most people worked. We easily forget a world without spreadsheets, word processors, email, and presentation products, and although Lotus and WordPerfect were the early innovators, Microsoft spread this technology wide and deep. For me, this was a giant exercise in change management—introducing an entire generation to a new way to work—but it was only the end of the beginning in my education in transformational leadership.

As it turned out, Microsoft Office was the appetizer. Xbox was the main course, presenting an opportunity to influence the way people played and how they experienced entertainment. To do that successfully required both adjusting perceptions about "gaming" and shifting the way people thought about interactive entertainment. The Xbox project changed the way Microsoft approached consumers creating an entrée into the larger entertainment world and staking a claim in the technological frontier of the living room.

Adding to these challenges, the project also required us to be entrepreneurs within a company of over 39,000 employees in over seventy countries and comprising businesses that ranged from operating systems to mission-critical enterprise applications to mice and keyboards.

Microsoft was a complex ecosystem, and the leaders of the Xbox enterprise, in particular the Chief Xbox Officer, had to learn how to benefit from that ecosystem while avoiding the traps and challenges it created. I think of this as "intrapreneurship," a word I didn't invent, but one that aptly describes our task.

Unbeknownst to me, my roles with Microsoft Office and Xbox expanded my repertoire, requiring a transformation from being a good business manager to being a respected business leader. These experiences stretched me from just expressing strong opinions to articulating an inspiring vision that could focus and energize thousands of people. Most importantly, I developed outstanding strategic skills and the ability to drive change in large, complex situations.

TO SEMIAHMOO WE GO

When I tell someone I worked on Xbox from the beginning, I usually get a response along the lines of "Wow, what a great opportunity" or "I bet your kids thought you were cool" or even "Can I have your autograph for my son?" In hindsight, I'm naturally very proud of what the Xbox team accomplished and thankful for the opportunity given to us at Microsoft, but in those first years of the project, I was not sure whether this was a career opportunity or career suicide. In the beginning, Xbox was the biblical equivalent of "formless and empty" and quickly escalated into a game of high stakes poker with billions of dollars and the company's reputation at stake. Every challenging strategy process begins

> Xbox was the biblical equivalent of "formless and empty" and quickly escalated into a game of high stakes poker with billions of dollars and the company's reputation at stake.

with a clear definition of the problem—and as it turns out, Xbox had more than its fair share.

Microsoft's bold foray into the video game business began in the spring of 1999 at the Semiahmoo Resort in a remote corner of Washington State. Over seventy executives, including all fifty-nine of the company's corporate vice presidents, were participating in a retreat for senior executives, a two-night, off-site event to discuss the state of the company, review key strategy and product initiatives, and set objectives for the coming fiscal year. Bill Gates and Steve Ballmer used this event to engage with the leadership group, build camaraderie across the group, and send specific messages to the team.

This was an annual event I loved to hate. I knew it was a good idea, and I enjoyed catching up with friends from across the company, but I always struggled with the artificiality of sitting in executive wingback chairs in a stuffy ballroom listening to presentations while people were actually catching up on email. The 1999 retreat included most of the typical off-site components—sit, listen, talk, eat—but that year a new process called Open Space was added to the event, allowing anyone to propose ideas that groups would discuss in breakout sessions. There were perhaps twenty topics proposed, including one from Bill Gates on a highly technical data structure issue, and people then "voted with their feet" to pick the topic where they would participate.

Rick Thompson, our Vice President of Hardware—think mice and keyboards—proposed the idea of Microsoft doing a video game console. Rick worked for me at the time, and at first blush, I thought this was one of the craziest ideas I'd heard. Rick's hardware job notwithstanding, Microsoft was a productivity software company through and through, and the idea that we would get involved in hardware, and entertainment hardware at that, seemed anathema to our mission. To my surprise, Bill decided this topic was more interesting than his own and joined us in one of the hotel rooms, complete with beds oddly rearranged so that we could conduct a meeting.

The premise behind Rick's proposal was to drive Microsoft's presence in the living room and prevent Sony and the PlayStation2 (PS2) from controlling computing outside of the business productivity world. As far as that went, I suppose you could say, "so far so good." And as it turned out, there were a number of groups within Microsoft doing their own game console "garage-shop" work in their free time, and they had divergent views on how to bring this vision to life. Following the retreat, Bill spent several months meeting with these teams to evaluate various ways to create a next-generation console using Microsoft DNA. By midsummer, he thought there was a technical plan that would work effectively, but he asked Steve Ballmer to determine if we could make a good business case for the project. Steve assigned Rick Thompson (and by extension, me) to firm up the product plan and create a business case for pursuing what was code named the Xbox project.

By autumn, Rick and a small team of vanguard Xboxers had explored a variety of go-to-market strategies and partnerships. They had solicited advice, guidance, and input from most of the existing console manufacturers, consumer electronics companies, and game publishers. We certainly received plenty of feedback, setting the stage for the first of many product-definition debates within the group, as well as with Bill Gates and Steve Ballmer.

The original concept called for Microsoft to design a reference platform for the hardware, produce the system software, and create a number of Xbox games. We would also manage the process of licensing the platform out to other game developers and collecting royalties from them as they created and sold games. The actual hardware would be manufactured and sold by other consumer electronics companies, following the basic Windows OEM model that had made Microsoft so successful.

Unfortunately, this model ran into two major problems: we couldn't find consumer electronics OEMs who would manufacture an Xbox console because the anticipated profit margins were too low or even negative. Likewise, our third-party game publishers, including companies like Electronic Arts (EA) and Activision, told us they would only develop for Xbox if we produced and priced the hardware and provided the marketing spend for the platform. As a final nail in the coffin, they were uninterested in a system that allowed multitasking like a PC; they wanted 100 percent of the console's resources available for game development.

Responding to this feedback, we presented a significantly different plan to Bill and Steve on December 21, 1999. Consistent with the original proposal, it called for the creation of a very powerful console, including a hard disk, based on a PC-like architecture. The team concluded that Microsoft needed to manufacture, market, and sell the hardware and the product should be a dedicated gaming console with virtually no general purpose capabilities. The plan also established a Herculean timetable that called for building the team, creating the product, designing and manufacturing the accessories, and developing a full slate of games for delivery by Christmas 2001. For good measure, we concluded we would lose roughly two billion dollars entering the market because our primary competitor would have a twelve- to eighteen-month head start.

In true Microsoft fashion, Bill and Steve approved the project and off we went with our Don Quixote quote book in hand, ready to tilt at windmills. Nobody could fault us for our ambition or courage.

THE VALENTINE'S DAY MASSACRE

Our strategic challenges began right at the foundations of the Xbox project, where there was no core agreement on our basic mission. If you had asked three people, "Why are you doing Xbox?" you would have gotten three different answers. Someone would have said, "Because we have to beat Sony in the living room" (whatever that meant). Another would have claimed that "we can build something that uses the power of the PC ecosystem to produce a better, totally redefined gaming experience." And still a third might have said, "Microsoft needs to branch out into other markets to drive growth and profit." While all of these statements were true to varying degrees, none of them satisfied the first step in the yet-to-be developed 3P Framework. They didn't state our purpose, the first element in developing and communicating a complete strategy to the team.

At that advanced stage of the project, I could not articulate a clearly defined mission for Xbox. The truth is that the thought never even crossed my mind. Thinking as a manager rather than as a leader, I was far too busy dealing with day-to-day crises to step back and actually survey the forest to establish a strategic approach to our problems. This lack of clarity created significant short-term and long-term issues for the team; building a complicated project on top of an unclear foundation is not a recipe for success. See Pisa, Leaning Tower of.

The official approval for Xbox in December 1999 didn't allay the doubts others had about our chosen approach. There were senior leaders in the company who thought the entire project was misguided and should be cancelled before it even got started. Bill and Steve heard many of these concerns, which gave rise to second thoughts of their own. On Valentine's Day 2000, less than two months after our initial approval, Steve called a senior leadership meeting to reevaluate our plan, largely precipitated by some heated email exchanges concerning the strategy.

This meeting included the four primary leaders of the Xbox project—J Allard, Ed Fries, Rick Thompson, and me. Also present were Bill Gates, Steve Ballmer, Rick Belluzzo, and a few other senior leaders from outside the Xbox team who had a stake in our work or cared personally about the gaming space. We later dubbed this meeting the "Valentine's Day Massacre" because it was originally scheduled as a one-hour meeting at the end of the day and ended up lasting over three hours, ruining a number of planned romantic evenings.

The meeting was held in the Microsoft board room in Building 8. Considering this was the headquarters of what many saw as the technologic evil empire of that era, Building 8 was rather small and nondescript. There was a receptionist but no visible security—a throwback to the days before 9/11. Finding the board room was quite the adventure. You had to know just the right progression of left and right turns to get there, and even then you might go right past it without noticing. Or you might stumble into Bill Gates's office, which was across the hall from the meeting room.

The room itself was quite small with a conference table that could comfortably seat twelve but holding SRO seating for about thirty people, assuming nobody wanted to be comfortable. It had no external windows—just glass facing out into an internal hallway, and even that window was usually covered with drapes. The whole claustrophobic effect was like entering a submarine, making it the perfect battle-worn

venue for many epic product reviews, budget discussions, and strategic debates. I'd been called "stupid" there more times than I care to
remember . . . and somehow I kept going back for more.

The meeting began in the usual dramatic fashion, with Bill arriv-
ing late and diving right into the middle of the conversation (literally
and figuratively), slamming his hand on the table, and yelling at me in
"clear terms" about the errors of our ways. The concerns ranged from
our deviation from the PC business and technical model, to the size
of the financial losses, to the confusion Xbox could create in the PC
games market. Most important, our plan, such as it was, went against
the grain of most lessons Microsoft had learned in its first twenty-five
years of success.

Understandably, anything that could disrupt the PC/Windows
ecosystem—the strategic and financial heart of Microsoft's business—
required something akin to tiptoeing through the tulips without
crushing any of the flowers. A long, unfocused debate ensued over
our plan's lack of strategic focus and clarity: Were we creating Xbox
to move the PC into the living room, or were we doing it to build a
living room business? Although I didn't realize it at the time, this was
my first hint that the Xbox project would come to be about managing
change—in the market and within Microsoft.

After a couple of hours of raised voices and more table pounding—this was an old-school Microsoft meeting, after all—I said,
"Look, if you don't want to do this, just say so. We all had other jobs
before this got started, and we can move back to doing other things if
that is what you want." The Xbox team's stance was simple: this is the
only way we can do this successfully, and if that doesn't fit with the
company's direction, let's cancel the project and move on. This incited
an unfocused discussion in the opposite direction about what would

happen in the marketplace if we did not do Xbox. In the end, we agreed that Xbox was important to the broader company strategy for a number of reasons, among them the necessity to compete with Sony in the living room. Not the crispest of answers, but at least an answer.

Steve asked Rick Belluzzo, my boss at the time, if he thought the current team was capable of doing this successfully. In many ways, this was an unfair question since the group was still forming, the leaders were largely untested at this scale, and important portions of the plan had yet to be written. To his enduring credit, Rick answered quickly and firmly that he trusted the team to get it done. In a moment that changed many of our lives, Steve concluded that the time for second guessing was over and gave the project the go-ahead. He and Bill agreed to provide strong support for the program and give us the opportunity to prove our plan.

True to their word, they remained strong, firm Xbox supporters through the good and especially through the bad of the early days of the project, and without that support, Xbox would not have survived. I often reflect that it is easy to criticize CEOs and leaders for decisions that turn out badly, and Bill and Steve have certainly been subject to their share of scrutiny. But I also believe that we mostly forget to give leaders credit when they make tough, even brave, decisions that turn out well and change the course of an industry. I will never forget Bill and Steve's leadership, and Rick's strong support, on that Valentine's Day.

Soon thereafter, Rick Thompson decided to leave Microsoft to work at a start-up he had helped fund, and I became the day-to-day leader of the Xbox project, a position we later called the Chief Xbox Officer. I have never been a gamer, and my selection as the leader had more to do with the fact that I already oversaw the PC games and hardware divisions, the businesses most relevant to the Xbox effort. Serendipity has a way of creating opportunity by putting us in a certain place at the right time. Ready or not, I was now in charge of a very complex project, one that would require equal combinations of creativity, strategic thinking, organizational skills, and no small amount of luck.

THE E3 FROM HELL

Every project of Xbox's scale has its up and downs—there is a rhythm of challenges, surprises, great work, and new obstacles that is associated with any complex endeavor. Building Xbox followed this pattern but involved at least one or two standard deviations worth of issues. To be fair, most of these wounds were self-inflicted, including a period where we reached a verbal agreement with a start-up company to utilize a set of custom chipsets, only to reverse our technical course less than a week later and select chips that were closer to "off-the-shelf" offerings from established companies.

This yo-yo decision making caused huge challenges with our partners but created even greater havoc within our own development teams. Given that we were literally building the team while we spec'd and developed the product, everyone had to deal with a complex maelstrom of changes every day. The only real constants we had were a ship date (November 8, 2001), a mantra to be bigger/faster/prettier than PS2, and a belief that adding a hard drive and an online component were critical to differentiating the product. And even that last item was a bit of fantasy since we had no concrete plan for implementing an online service.

We compounded the challenges associated with an unclear purpose by not developing a comprehensive management approach that was shared by the entire team. As the leader of the team, I failed to develop or encourage a cohesive culture or a decision-making process. This missing piece, the principles layer in the 3P Framework, made it very difficult to create a successful plan of attack.

As the original Xbox team grew, it began to feel more and more like running the United Nations. We had a core set of people from the PC games group, some mice and keyboard hardware engineers, networking and operating systems experts from the Windows team, and a large number of people who joined Microsoft from the games industry. We also built a retail sales and operations team, largely from scratch, to work directly with retailers and our manufacturing partners.

We hired an exceptionally smart and passionate group, but they all came from different operating cultures and were motivated by different things. The team was not very cohesive, had trouble communicating with each other, and struggled to make decisions that cut across parts of the organization. And almost every important decision cut across multiple groups in the business. To be clear, a group of Type-A personalities with a dysfunctional culture trying to achieve a very difficult, complicated task is not a recipe for success, especially when the leadership was not strong enough to organize the team properly. I certainly learned about the importance of principles the hard way . . .

Lacking any semblance of a clear strategic framework, the project moved along in a herky-jerky fashion, with the team making up for the inherent strategic and cultural misalignment with inspired ideas, will power, and no small amount of blind faith. As we moved into 2001, I knew that shipping the console and game portfolio on time and at sufficient quality would be a difficult challenge.

On the hardware front, we quickly realized there weren't any off-the-shelf-parts, as each component required just enough tweaks to turn them into custom parts. This was especially true with our graphics chip from NVIDIA. We were using a permutation of their latest, greatest, next-generation design, which is another way of saying we were constantly missing our schedules. Even something as simple as the DVD drive was problematic—we had firmware challenges that almost slipped the entire project.

On the software side, developers were using PCs to create new game concepts or to port games from the PS2, but they struggled to take advantage of the hard drive and couldn't optimize their games since we hadn't shipped them final development machines. While the team was working flat out, there was no way to solve our issues with more resources. In fact, adding more people to the project would have made this three-ring circus even more difficult to manage.

Rumors of these problems circulated through the game community, and that traumatic May 16 launch presentation at E3 confirmed we were in real trouble. Our approach to the show mirrored how our organization functioned. I arrived for rehearsals the day before the event only to discover that we were not even ready for a walk-through. Somehow, we were so preoccupied with other tasks leading up to the event that we forgot we actually had to produce a show. Rather than having one person clearly in charge, we had a very committed collection of production, events, and PR people working very hard to try to pull everything together. I should have put a stop to the insanity, but I dove right in and tried to help with the writing of the script, the selection of demos and presenters, and the overall messaging for the day. After many hours and at least two outlines of an "order of show," I went back to my hotel at 2 a.m. and began (again) to write my speech.

Upon arrival early the next morning, I realized that no magic fairy dust had descended on the venue overnight—we were still scrambling to make final decisions. Beyond the symbolic failure of the product to turn on, one of our demos from industry leader Electronic Arts consisted of a pirate ship continually running itself into the rocks—one of those iconic yet inauspicious metaphors that are funny in hindsight but demoralizing in the present.

Our problems, unbelievably, did not end at the presentation. Our booth at the convention center was equally reflective of the state of affairs across the team, and my presentation at a panel discussion with the heads of Sony and Nintendo was not my finest hour. Our messaging was incoherent, our keynote speech was disorganized, our demos did not work, and our most highly touted game, Halo, looked terrible and was no fun to play. Other than that, it was a great party.

To be fair to the team and myself, everyone worked tirelessly to get us through the show, and history would demonstrate that winning E3 had little impact on who ultimately won in the marketplace. Nevertheless, I left the convention later that week anxious and demoralized with serious doubts about my own leadership and decision-making skills.

Not long after the E3 debacle, Peter Moore flew up to Redmond to pay me a visit to discuss the status of the Xbox project. Peter was then President of Sega of America, one of the few Japanese game developers who had pledged to support the Xbox launch. In fact, Peter's appearance on stage during our E3 presentation was by far the highlight of the event. His message to me that day was pretty simple.

To paraphrase politely, he told me their research indicated we were dead in the water with consumers, losing traction with developers, and at risk of getting no shelf space for our products at retail. While this wasn't exactly the pep talk I needed, it confirmed my own fears and suspicions.

The harsh reality was that our launch date was less than six months away, and I was not sure we were going to make it.

HITTING ROCK BOTTOM

I am a positive thinker. I have always had an optimistic outlook on life and confidence in my abilities. But E3 rocked me to the core, a cold, lonely place I'd only visited once before in my life. I could have rationalized this by saying that the team did a poor job, that the task was impossible anyway, or that this was just normal growing pains for an ambitious, risky start-up venture. But behind all those excuses rested a simple truth: I was doing a poor job providing leadership and direction to the team, and my inexperience in product development was showing in a way that was seriously detrimental to the project.

I was definitely giving 120 percent effort and doing my best to make decisions and keep the team moving forward, but my natural tendency to dive in and solve problems myself was actually working against me. I never did the challenging work required of strong leaders—I never stepped back and orchestrated the team around a coordinated strategy. Without that foundation, all of my other leadership qualities were insufficient to carry the day.

On May 24, 2001, just a week after the disastrous E3 showing, I suffered through another difficult set of meetings lasting well past the dinner hour. When I finally came home, Pauline and I had a long conversation that lasted late into the night. For too long, I had been overwhelmed at work and permanently distracted at home. Pauline was essentially raising three young, active children as a single mom and overseeing the building of a new house. She had always been supportive, but her message came through loud and clear: "We miss you in the family." For me, this was the true definition of hitting rock bottom.

After she went to bed, I sat down in the dark in our playroom to write the following email to Rick Belluzzo:

From: *Robert (Robbie) Bach*
Sent: *Friday, May 25, 2001 2:02 AM*
To: *Rick Belluzzo*
Subject: *My Status and Xbox*
Importance: *High*

This is not going to be an easy email to write—and frankly, I've postponed doing it several times. The short summary is that my direct involvement in Xbox needs to end—and sooner than either of us would like. I think this is both in my best interests and the best interests of Microsoft. That is the cliff notes. . . . here's the full story. . . .

First, I want to say that I'm intensely proud of what the team has accomplished over the last 12 months. We've gone from being a "nobody" in this area, to being considered seriously with both Nintendo and Sony. The team has put its heart and soul into making this happen, and they've done an amazing job. Even with all of the stupid curve balls we've been thrown, we are right on the cusp of shipping a very strong product, along with some great games. The road ahead is far from certain (see below), but we've put ourselves into position to be successful.

Second, I want to thank you, Steve, and Bill, for the confidence you placed in the team. You really have given us the resources and the leeway to get Xbox started and to build something of value. For myself, I often reflect on the fact that I have the best job in the company, and usually that is because of the flexibility and responsibility you've shown us. I've probably learned more in the last 12 months than I did in the prior 5 years combined. For that, I am very grateful.

Third, unfortunately with all that said, I'm not the right guy to lead this team going forward. This really boils down to the fact that some areas of the project are severely screwed up and I'm not the right guy to fix them. To wit:

1. *In Japan, we need to replace [the leadership] and really start over with the organization. I should have done this 6 months ago. This requires someone who has the capacity (and desire) to spend a ton of time in Japan—including probably being based there for a few months—and I just don't have this in me.*

2. *Back at home, I've let my desire to keep the project on track for this fall get in the way of managing nVidia in the proper way. We now have ourselves stuck in a very awkward corner, and I don't have the right relationship with Jensen to fix this.*

3. *I'm dismayed by my team's lack of discipline—around spending habits, around showing good judgement [sic] about appropriate behavior, and about general management skills. These are all signs of a team that is not being managed effectively—and that starts with and reflects directly back on me.*

4. *Fixing these kinds of problems requires someone with a fresh outlook and someone with a clean slate who can implement change quickly. I'm not that person.*

Finally—and most importantly—I'm failing at managing the balance between my job and my personal life. As much as I love the excitement, the intellectual challenge, and the learning I get at work, none of it is worth losing my family and friends over. As it stands now, work takes 110% of my energy starting at 7am in the morning and going until 7pm at night. By the time I spend time with our children, I have no energy left to spend with my wife. Pauline and I have been married for almost 16 years, and I want our relationship to be even stronger for the next 16 years. The job (or at least the way I'm doing it) is pulling me from this, and my family is more important to me than anything else in the world.

I started this email by saying that I'd postponed writing it for a while. The reason for the postponement is simple: I've made a firm commitment to you and SteveB to see this project through to success, and I gave the same commitment to the rest of the team. That commitment and sense of responsibility have prevented me from proposing my departure sooner. But none of those commitments is as important as the one I gave to Pauline and our kids. I'm not a quitter by nature, but I think a change would be good for both MS and me.

There's never a good time for stuff like this, and I'm sure this is no better than any other time—perhaps worse. I'm certainly willing to continue leading Xbox until you/we figure out a transition strategy with a specific person to replace me. But the thinking behind that process needs to start, and I need to begin ramping down on my emotional and intellectual connection to Xbox. That is the only way I'm going to be able to live up to the big commitments I have at home.

Sorry to dump this on you over email. Today was a long hard day and I needed to get this off my chest.

Thanks for listening. . . .

Robbie

———— ⏻ ————

At the end of May, 2001, the Xbox console launch was in real jeopardy: partners doubted our viability, the game portfolio was anemic, the team was fried, and I was resigning as CXO. Whether you are running a business venture, reviewing a government program, or just evaluating the status of a project, this prognosis is the textbook definition of a "problem statement." Fortunately for the team and Microsoft, a reset—a dramatic change in approach and strategy—was just over the horizon. A return to common sense was in the offing.

At the end of May, 2001, the Xbox console launch was in real jeopardy: partners doubted our viability, the game portfolio was anemic, the team was fried, and I was resigning as CXO.

3

STEPPING BACK TO MOVE FORWARD

Rick Belluzzo refused to let me quit. After an urgent and somewhat panicked early-morning phone exchange, he listened to my concerns and then challenged me to attack the problem on both the professional and personal levels. Rick was wonderful at providing perspective and enabled me to sort through the various problems in a dispassionate way. It was one of those meetings where you left feeling like a load had been lifted from your shoulders, but you weren't really sure where it had gone. He did offer some real, practical solutions, both in the short term and the long term, that ultimately changed my trajectory as a manager and leader. He left the company not long after the launch of Xbox, but he played an important, if sometimes hidden, role in the project's success, and he enabled me to become the kind of leader the team sorely needed.

The Xbox launch date was less than six months away, so I had to kick into high gear on all fronts. Professionally, I stepped up my game, determined to get the team to the finish line and establish a beachhead in the video game wars. At the same time, Rick introduced me to Jack Fitzpatrick and Anne Francis at the Family Business Resource Center, conveniently located in Topeka, Kansas. I suppose it would be cliché to say that like Dorothy, I found myself when I came to Kansas, but there is great truth in that statement.

Over a number of weeks, Jack and Anne forced me to step back from my work and answer a whole host of fundamental questions, involving Pauline in the process in a meaningful way. I wrote pages and pages in response to their queries, including my family history, a description of three significant people in my life, and my plans for retirement, which, at age thirty-nine, seemed a bit premature.

Sitting down in front of a blank screen and writing a self-description, including your plans for the future and why you need help, might sound easy. Try it some time, and you will discover the true meaning of writer's block. As difficult as these questions were to answer, the process forced me to think about my career, my relationship with Pauline, and the need to bring balance back to my life. I reread my responses recently and found an enlightening reminder of who I am and what I want to become—including a desire to someday write a book.

TRANSFORMATIONAL CHANGE

These introspective exercises enabled me to reflect on my upbringing, understand how my experiences had influenced my character, and consider both my natural and cultivated talents. I saw that I already possessed some of the most important tools necessary to negotiate the challenges I faced at Microsoft. Although some of these were innate strengths, I came by others the hard way, and that journey is part of the story of transformational change.

In the movies, there is usually a dramatic build-up to some life-altering event that forms the crux of a dilemma or the dénouement to a suspenseful drama. You can feel it in the plot, in the emotions of the characters, and even in the music and lighting. The director wants you edging forward further and further in your seat (or sinking back deeper and deeper) until you are ready for that big moment. Yet early in my life things didn't work that way. I grew up in a normal and stable environment, enjoying the support of four siblings, good neighborhood friends, and plenty of Mom's home cooking. My days were predictable—go to school, study a bit (although not really very much), play sports, eat dinner with the family, repeat.

My life had a regular rhythm, consistent like a drumbeat. Then one night in the spring of my seventh grade, my mom told me we were moving from Wisconsin to North Carolina at the end of the summer. Just like that. No suspense, no build-up, not even an explanation. Your life is going to change. Next.

> No suspense, no build-up, not even an explanation. Your life is going to change. Next.

My body was experiencing major change, too. I grew almost eight inches that year and never really knew it was happening except when I noticed my bell bottom pants had become "high waters." Plaid bell bottoms were never really a good look anyway, and for a guy, showing more leg did not enhance the experience. The bigger problem with all of the growth was the effect it had on my back. Literally in the span of a weekend, I went from a seemingly healthy, athletic boy in puberty to someone whose back hurt so much he could barely sit down. My doctor initially thought it was a minor issue, and whenever the pain subsided, I was inclined to agree. Thankfully, my mother was more skeptical and kept searching for answers to what she knew deep down was a real problem.

My family is serious about its sports, in part because we are competitive to a fault, and in part because we find real joy in the sport itself. My siblings were accomplished athletes in track and field, tennis, and swimming, and while basketball was always my passion, I was the top-ranked tennis player in Wisconsin and at one point, in the top fifty nationally. In a most unexpected way, sports saved me from a life of physical pain and struggle.

In my mom's pursuit of answers to my back problems, she reached out to a neighbor whose son also happened to be a highly ranked tennis player. Gary Taxman had back issues that were eventually diagnosed as scoliosis—a serious curvature of the spine, which, if left untreated, can cause permanent pain and organ damage. My mom arranged for us to meet with Gary's doctor.

Dr. Walter Blount was not your ordinary doctor, and this was no typical appointment. He was retiring from practice and no longer taking new cases, but he was going to a tournament to see Gary play competitive tennis in the back brace Dr. Blount had pioneered to treat scoliosis. My mom hauled me down to the park to watch Gary play, hoping I would be able to spend a few minutes with Dr. Blount.

We all have memories burned into our brains, ones we can never forget. My first handshake with Dr. Blount is amongst my most vivid memories. He was certainly a kindly man, a bit frail in appearance with his hand shaking due to Parkinson's disease. We chatted about nothing in particular, as his attention was clearly on his star pupil. So we watched Gary play for a few minutes, which was really quite remarkable given the bulk of a full-body brace designed to straighten out his malformed spine. I was thinking, *How strange to see a funny-looking, handicapped kid playing tennis*. Little did I know.

Dr. Blount turned to me and said, "Take off your shirt and bend over," as if doing that in a public park while watching a tennis match was a completely natural thing to request of someone you'd just met. Of course, I did what he asked, and it took him about a minute to make a diagnosis. I had kyphosis, a disease related to scoliosis, which curves the spine forward (almost forty degrees forward in my case). Dr. Blount paused for a moment, looked at my mom, and accepted me as a new patient, probably his last. Just like that, my life changed dramatically for the second time in one summer. One minute, I was watching a supposedly handicapped kid play tennis, and the next minute I was the one with the handicap, poised to get fitted for a back brace. No suspense, no build-up, not even an explanation. Your life is going to change. Next.

While the eighth grade seems a bit early for a defining moment in one's life, the forced move to North Carolina combined with the addition of my "Milwaukee" brace, as it was called, altered my outlook on life. Moving from a lily-white existence in a northern suburb to an integrated school district complete with forced busing in Winston-Salem was quite the culture shock. Wearing a back brace twenty-three hours a day did not help my self-esteem, to say nothing of my path to social integration.

The brace wrapped a full-leather girdle around my waist, a metal bar straight in front of my chest, and two additional bars along my back. The bars attached at the top to a ring that circled my neck with a chinrest in the front. I would slide into it from the back, tighten a screw at the back of the neck ring, and cinch up the girdle with a strap to tighten it around my waist. I learned quickly what it meant to be different. I think the problem was mostly of my own making, but I definitely went from an active social life to one filled with hours of self-reflection and loneliness.

My mom and dad were devout Catholics, and I was raised with a set of religious beliefs and a form of worship that I still practice today. Nevertheless, my mom taught me more about faith—in God and myself—during that difficult period than I could ever have learned in any church, congregation, or synagogue. She devoted herself to keeping me on course, getting up early in the morning to help me with my back exercises. She picked me up after school, and she filled in a social gap since I was struggling to make friends. At first, she took me to play golf, a sport that was new to me but which became a lifelong passion. She also encouraged me to relearn how to play tennis from scratch, as each movement was now totally different. At her urging, I applied myself in school, and with the help of my dad, who was a math whiz, I caught up to the other kids in the advanced classes in which I'd been placed. In short, she gave me the courage to believe in myself, to ignore my back issues, to deal with a new life, and to find faith in the simple things each day. That strength of faith is amongst the gifts I hold most precious today.

Much of what I learned during that time about faith in God, the importance of family, trust in my own abilities, and perseverance gave rise to a steady flow of serendipitous surprises, including the opportunity to play varsity tennis at the University of North Carolina (coincidentally following in the footsteps of Gary Taxman). As I reflected on this history with Jack and Anne, I realized that my God-given talents and the skills that I'd developed through experience were the tools I needed to lead the Xbox team through its own transformative change. The first steps in that process had to begin with me—reframing how I viewed my past trials, reshaping my personal life, and rethinking my approach to leadership were all pre-requisites for transforming the Xbox business.

THE TRIUMPH OF PRACTICAL ADVICE

In the spring of 2002, with Xbox launched in each of the major markets, I took some time out to complete the work begun with Jack Fitzpatrick and Anne Francis. Pauline and I made a two-day pilgrimage to see them in Topeka. There, in the quiet setting of a Kansas farm, I learned a great deal more about myself and developed a deeper respect and love for my wife. I began to understand what she was dealing with as a result of my dysfunction. At one point, I told Jack that I felt guilty about leaving Microsoft in the lurch if I left the company. He gave me some of the best advice I've ever received. "Boy, that is the stupidest thing I've ever heard," he said. "If you want to leave, you should leave. How to replace you is not your problem; that is Rick Belluzzo's problem, and you should let him do his job. But if what you are really telling me is that you are frustrated with your own failings, then get over your guilt and angst and get on with leading the team." Sometimes what you need is a good knock to the head.

Thanks to our work with Jack and Anne and a ten-week sabbatical that followed, I rebuilt my approach to leading the team and managing my personal life, allowing me to run the group more successfully and build deeper, lasting relationships with my wife and children. Whether that was a midlife crisis or not I will never know, but I was surprised how quickly I pivoted from frustrated resignation to resolute determination once I approached life's challenges with a more common-sense attitude. Jack and Anne's basic message combined practical, life-management techniques with healthy elements of empowerment and accountability.

> Whether that was a midlife crisis or not I will never know, but I was surprised how quickly I pivoted from frustrated resignation to resolute determination once I approached life's challenges with a more common-sense attitude.

On the professional front, they challenged me to embrace the problems we faced in the Xbox business, including the dysfunctional nature of the team, and take responsibility for making changes rather than letting the problems change me. As a result, I committed to leading the team in a more disciplined and effective manner, and I promised to make significant changes at work in order to balance my business and home lives.

To that end, I restructured my day to be at home until the kids were off to school and to get home in time for coaching, attending games, or sharing a family dinner. I think people were a bit taken aback the first time I got up and left a staff meeting so I could coach my daughter's basketball team, but over time, people got the message. My new-found boundaries around family time forced everyone to be more efficient because the work day had an official end and decisions needed to be made. This change implicitly gave other leaders permission to recognize that their personal lives were important and that creating better work-life balance made them better employees and teammates.

I gained better control of my time by instituting a new rule regarding requests for out-of-town meetings: I required my team to plan travel nine months in advance, refusing to make trips that suddenly showed up on my calendar. This approach had a number of positive effects. People placed a greater value on my time and only requested me for important meetings. They were also much more thoughtful about my itineraries, packing them with higher-impact, more significant events that brought more value to the business.

The "because-we-can" meetings also went away, and people that weren't thoughtful or didn't plan ahead learned the consequences rather quickly. Other leaders emerged in the organization to take some of the meetings I declined, and that ultimately built a stronger bench within our management team. Finally, and most importantly, it allowed Pauline and me to make our own plans and ensured that I could support the family in the way they deserved. These changes and the grace, patience, and steadiness of my wife enabled us to live a busy, enjoyable family life and raise our three great kids together, even as I continued to lead the Xbox team. And we still talk with Jack and Anne regularly today . . .

DEFINING SUCCESS

While I was finding my footing and establishing a foundation for leadership, the rest of the Xbox team picked up the ball and ran with it. In fact, the E3 conference fiasco served as a warning siren that mobilized everyone as no leader could have. Key individuals on the team stepped up and took charge of various groups, literally willing us to the finish line.

The hardware and manufacturing teams, despite some difficult technical hurdles and logistics challenges, somehow produced 1.3 million consoles, which we sold quickly, particularly in the US. The software team made it easier for developers to create great games on Xbox and enabled consumers to see and feel the raw power of the product. The Bungie team, whose signature game had struggled at E3, finished their development cycle with miraculous skill creating *Halo: Combat Evolved*, one of the industry's enduring and most valuable franchises. And the sales and marketing teams built a distribution channel and brand from the ground up that proved Microsoft could sell products to consumers.

By March 2002, the Xbox team had pulled off what had seemed improbable to most in the industry only nine months earlier: Xbox was winning customers across North America, Europe, and the Asia Pacific region. Over the next four years, Xbox achieved a market share ranging from 20 to 25 percent in most markets, except in Japan and Spain, where the product struggled mightily. Although we badly trailed Sony's PS2, Xbox was considered more of a success than Nintendo's GameCube, even though our share numbers were similar and Nintendo was highly profitable. Given our lack of experience in the business, people were surprised by our ability to innovate, produce interesting game experiences, and gain the support of most publishers. Against tremendous odds, we succeeded in building that much desired beachhead for Microsoft in the video game industry.

At the same time, there were problems that had to be addressed: balky DVD drives slowed manufacturing, a mediocre launch in Europe hurt our momentum outside of the United Kingdom, complaints about disk scratching and a weak game lineup killed our business in Japan, and a shortage of high-quality games beyond Halo raised some doubts among the game *cognoscenti*. Our online game service, Xbox Live, did not ship for another year, and Electronic Arts refused to support that service at launch. These potholes along the way enabled Sony to build a huge business before some of our key differentiators were even available or viable.

Our P&L was, of course, the ultimate measure of success, and our market-share beachhead came at tremendous cost. The original forecast for Xbox called for an investment (a code word for loss) of roughly two billion dollars during the first generation of the product. In fact, Xbox lost somewhere between five and seven billion dollars, depending on how you did the accounting, a number that frustrated many in the company and was widely criticized by members of the investment community.

To complete this evaluation of the original product, we had a serious problem with priorities. Xbox had no shortage of key initiatives, and the team spent its first twenty-four months in perpetual firefighting mode. The most important priority was always the next deadline, and since we were not crisp in making decisions, those deadlines often slipped, creating even more of a crisis atmosphere.

As an example, we knew from the beginning that online gaming was going to be an important element in our Xbox strategic plan, but we never managed to prioritize the required set of decisions high enough to get the project rolling in a timely fashion. In the interim, our users held Halo parties, where they wired four Xbox consoles together with Ethernet cables to play "Halo online." This demonstrated both their excitement about online gaming and our inability to deliver it in a timely fashion. While postponing the online portion of the project may have been necessary in any event, the delay was really caused by our inability to focus on the most important issues facing the project.

This absence of clear priorities affected the team and each of us individually. In the theatre of the absurd, I found myself one night sitting on a chair in front of my TV with an Xbox prototype on the floor. My task for the evening was to insert every one of our family DVDs to determine if the Xbox could play the TV shows and movies correctly. Press button with foot. Insert DVD. Close drive with foot. Check screen to ensure the DVD played. Press button to eject DVD. Repeat one hundred times. While I was proud to be the leading DVD tester in the group, I should have been appalled by the prioritization implicit in the CXO doing bulk DVD testing.

As I look back on it, I don't think of the original Xbox in terms of success or failure. There was certainly plenty of both to go around. Instead, my net takeaway is that the business somehow survived a hellishly difficult incubation. That survival, that precarious perch on the edge of the marketplace, can be attributed to three achievements: the creation of the Halo franchise, the eventual success of the Xbox Live business, and the fostering of strong relationships with key publishing partners like Electronic Arts and Activision. Supporting these milestones was the company's willingness to invest far beyond our original projections, and probably far beyond the actual competitive threat from Sony. And perhaps more important than all of those achievements were the effort and commitment of individuals dedicated to doing whatever it took to succeed.

THE COMMON SENSE OF 3-30-300

When I left for my sabbatical in mid-2002, it wasn't clear if I was going to come back to Microsoft, much less Xbox. Our recent visit to Topeka was still very much on my mind, demanding that I sift through the rubble of my Xbox leadership experience. While my resignation letter and trip to Topeka were never discussed outside of Rick Belluzzo's office, I imagine there were many in the industry and some on my own team who thought "sabbatical" was a synonym for "leaving soon."

There were times when I might have agreed with them, but during my time off, I was reminded of a stark, naked truth: I am a hyper-competitive person who really, really hates to lose, and I certainly am not a quitter. After a very quiet ten weeks spent with my family moving into our new house, I came back rejuvenated and ready to tackle the next phase of building the Xbox business. I knew this would require difficult decisions, a long-term commitment to the project, and a renewed concept of leadership.

The market reality was equally stark: despite two years of intensive, exhausting work, Xbox was far from out of the deep, dark woods. I knew our success had to rely on more than a collection of great individuals: we had to create a team with a shared culture and a unified strategy. Sony's dominant market share gave them large advantages across many parts of the business. Publishers were still focusing their first and best efforts on the PS2 platform, and retailers gave them better shelf space and merchandising. The Xbox console was not designed to sell profitability at the required price points, and we lacked sufficient scale to make up for those losses in other parts of the business. Driving Xbox off the beachhead into the mainstream consumer space meant redesigning the business from top to bottom. To do that, the Xbox Leadership Team (naturally, in Microsoft's love for acronyms, the XLT) needed a better approach to strategy development.

While continuing to manage and sell the original version of Xbox, we began thinking about the future of the business and our next-generation console, code named Xenon. Elements of the Xenon plan took shape shortly after the original Xbox shipped. The team explored new chipsets, which would become the core brains for our next major upgrade some four to five years away. This extended lead time presented an important challenge to the leadership team. We barely had our act together running the current business and yet needed to provide long-term strategic direction to the silicon-chip vanguards of the Xenon project. After far too many meetings at which we were asked to make important early decisions about the project without any real strategic context, we called an offsite to address the fundamental questions surrounding our Xenon strategy. The Xbox team was going through its own midlife crisis, and in my new mode of proactive leadership, I knew we desperately needed to reshape our entire identity and approach.

In February of 2003, the XLT got together over two days at the Salish Lodge, a rustic mountain retreat perched on top of a cliff over-looking a beautiful waterfall along the Snoqualmie River. The scenic beauty stood in sharp contrast to the shape of the management team and our approach to leadership. We were more like the rocks at the bottom of the falls than the serene river above. And the water just seemed to keep pounding us. We ensconced ourselves in a loft perched above the bar, which like the Microsoft board room was a bit cramped and hot in more ways than one. We had plenty of brains, passion, commitment, and ego, but those alone would prove insufficient for the challenges we faced.

> We were more like the rocks at the bottom of the falls than the serene river above. And the water just seemed to keep pounding us.

Like most retreats, we had an agenda designed to help us work through the broader issues our team faced, which in the case of the XLT, was improving how we worked together and making more timely decisions. The leadership was a microcosm of the Xbox team, representing a variety of viewpoints, approaches to products, and cultural beliefs—yet another instance of the United Nations effect.

Unfortunately, like the Security Council at the UN, the XLT was not a very effective leadership group. Instead of establishing a strategic architecture enabling our teams to make more decisions themselves, we allowed most issues—some important and some not—to bubble up to the XLT. There we debated the merits, often without reaching a concrete conclusion. In fact, more often than not, our so-called decisions amounted to asking the team to gather more data, rethink the issue, and come back to us with another proposal. J Allard called this "sending them back to the river to find another rock." Like our existence at the bottom of the metaphorical falls, this rock-finding process was intensely unsatisfying for all involved.

In our conference room at the Salish, we did all of the appropriate team-building exercises designed to break down the walls that divided the leadership team. As examples, we went through an exercise to share something about ourselves that others in the group did not know, and one unplanned exercise left us vacuuming and cleaning up the bar in pajamas at two in the morning. Thankfully, Facebook did not exist, or several of us might have been sent to the Human Resources team for "feedback."

All of this group engagement was interesting, useful, and even amusing—but by the second day, we clearly needed a breakthrough on the fundamental question: How could we build a Xenon strategy that would free the team to drive decisions with less involvement from the XLT? With great passion, J Allard outlined a new approach by urging the XLT to write down the core concepts of our strategy, allowing the rest of the team to build a structure around that framework. His proposal involved the creation of a three-page document defining the primary elements of our Xenon strategy. Based on this short document, the rest of the team would create longer documents defining the specifics of the plan without the XLT's day-to-day involvement.

J's concept became known as 3/30/300—a plan that consisted of a three-page document defining overall strategy, a thirty-page document breaking that strategy down into components for each team, and a three-hundred-page document that laid out the specific features and capabilities across the project. While I'm not aware of this terminology appearing in any business or strategy textbook, the approach appealed to the XLT because it was based on good common sense. I know J had used elements of this approach before, but this represented the first discussion he and I had with the rest of the leadership team around what evolved into the 3P Framework.

While there are many reasons for Xenon's ultimate success as the award-winning product Xbox 360, the common-sense nature of the 3/30/300 concept and the formation of the 3P Framework were critical steps in enabling the team to reshape and refocus itself. Pivoting a large, intricate ecosystem in mid-stream is a difficult task even in the best of situations. By definition, battleships do not pivot. But changing the direction of the struggling, money-losing Xbox group and creating a high-performance team in the process were the XLT's ultimate accomplishments, and perhaps my most important contributions to the Xbox business. This is the dynamic and transformative power of the 3P Framework at work.

4

SETTING THE GROUND RULES

Before every baseball game, the managers for each team come out of the dugout and meet with the umpires at home plate. I'm sure they talk about what they had for dinner the night before or what movie they watched . . . but technically, they are supposed to exchange line-up cards and discuss the unique rules associated with playing in that particular ballpark. In similar fashion, establishing a 3P Framework begins by defining the foundation of the strategy, the purpose and principle-based ground rules upon which priorities and eventual action plans will be built.

As the CXO, I took the assignment to lay out these core rules in the Xenon "three-pager." Naturally, there was no free time in my day-to-day schedule to write such an important document, so as history would have it, the core three-page document for Xenon was largely written on an Alaska Airlines flight from Cabo San Lucas to Seattle. The distractions provided by a golf weekend, enhanced by a thirty-foot putt on the last hole to win some money from my golf buddy John, enabled me to step back from the Xbox fray and clearly and objectively consider the future of Xenon.

After a four-hour flight home, I had a good first draft completed. We reviewed and debated that draft twice at XLT meetings over the following weeks, and on April 2, 2003, I published the Xenon three-page memo to the XLT, Bill Gates, Steve Ballmer, and a few other Microsoft senior executives. J Allard and I subsequently met with about fifty key leaders across the Xenon project and walked them through the document in great detail to ensure that the team was fully in sync and on board. In effect, this was our 3P Framework for Xenon even though we didn't use those terms at the time. Good architectural designs begin with a great foundation; likewise, good strategic frameworks begin with a strong declaration of purpose.

> Good architectural designs begin with a great foundation; likewise, good strategic frameworks begin with a strong declaration of purpose.

PURPOSE-BUILT

When I work with companies or nonprofits, and the topic of strategy comes up, I often ask them the simple question: "What is your purpose?" In most cases, I get a vague, ill-defined explanation or one that wanders from topic to topic. Sometimes I just get a long pause accompanied by a "What do you mean?" look. And yet my experience tells me that this is an absolutely critical question that must be answered crisply and consistently.

As an example, I'm on the Board of Directors for Sonos, the industry leader in wireless speakers and audio systems—the Internet's hi-fi for your home. If you ask anyone at Sonos to summarize the purpose of the company, he or she will inevitably say something like, "to fill every room in every house with all of the world's music." Nobody at Sonos has ever heard of the 3P Framework, but through strong leadership, their official mission "to fill every home with music" defines the foundation on which the company has built its entire strategy.

Another example strikes closer to home. Bill Gates and Paul Allen defined a powerful, motivating purpose early on at Microsoft: "A computer on every desk and in every home, running Microsoft software." This mantra was used in PR, speeches, company meetings, employee orientations, and other venues as the guiding light for all the work at the company. It motivated employees and focused the company's efforts incredibly effectively through the late 1990s. Since that time, Microsoft has struggled to redefine its overall purpose in a way that encompasses the full breadth of its businesses while continuing to motivate its teams and guide strategy.

Even if a purpose is well chosen, at some point, a renovation may be required. These midlife crises place companies in a very vulnerable position, as the revised purpose must provide new, lasting direction while still bridging from the strengths of the past. IBM is one of the better-known companies to make such a transition, albeit in fits and starts, as their focus migrated from hardware to enterprise software and services. By contrast, you would be hard pressed to identify a purpose for companies like GM, Yahoo, Sony, Hewlett-Packard, or Best Buy, all of whom have struggled with multiple redefinitions of their direction in the last five years.

In most cases, the purpose statement can be a pithy, motivational phrase or sentence like those from Sonos or Microsoft. This tagline approach has the advantage of being inspirational and memorable, thus lending itself to broad communications and effectiveness at many levels of an organization. Of course, it runs the risk of feeling too promotional or too broad. In some circumstances, it may be appropriate to have a slightly longer statement in favor of clarity and preciseness. Either way, people must be able to view the purpose statement as the rock on which the organization's strategy is built.

In a for-profit context, you might ask why the purpose statement doesn't resolve down to "we exist to make money." In my view of strategy, making money is a metric of success rather than an explicit purpose. Clearly an effective corporate strategy should lead to above-average market share and profits, but to provide those returns to shareholders, you must have a goal more fundamental and more aspirational than just making money.

Writing a purpose statement that enables this level of clarity is surprisingly difficult. While I was jetting from Cabo San Lucas to Seattle, I wanted to write an anthem for Xenon that was crisp, inspirational, and informative, but I quickly realized that ad slogans sound cheesy, and long, descriptive paragraphs generate no buzz or excitement. Being something of a left-brain thinker, I chose the latter approach and created a long sentence followed by paragraphs that explained the meaning of each portion of the purpose statement.

The Xenon three-pager we ultimately published incorporated what I now call purpose and principles into one statement. Although it did not happen in time for the Xenon work, separating these two strategic elements into distinct concepts makes purpose statements easier to create and more focused. It also enables an appropriate level of detail in the principles portion of the strategy.

To demonstrate this effect, I've redrafted the original document I presented to the Microsoft team, separating it into a crisp purpose statement and a longer statement of principles.

Xenon Purpose Statement: Xenon brings innovative forms of gaming and interactive entertainment to more living rooms than ever before.

This new purpose statement represented a departure from the original Xbox, whose ill-defined mission concentrated solely on gaming, and in particular on what we called "hardcore" gamers. At a technical level, the game in the disk drive of the original Xbox completely controlled the console, limiting its usefulness for other forms of entertainment. We also optimized all of the specifications to enable developers and producers to create powerful games for the expert gamer, including the coolest visuals, the biggest explosions, and the most realistic action in the industry. Our task was to prove to serious gamers that we understood their needs and passions and that Xbox should be an important part of their gaming experience. We entered the video game business to achieve a central role in the living room, but the original Xbox assumed that this dominance began with gaming and only gaming. Some journalists called this a "Trojan-horse" strategy—a deceptive, negative connotation that I would never acknowledge then, but upon reflection, I realize was an apt description of our approach.

With Xenon, we concluded that broadening our audience was a vital task. To be successful, Xenon had to drive significantly higher volume—roughly double what we had achieved with the original Xbox—and we didn't believe we could do that by competing with Sony and Nintendo solely in the gaming space. Consequently, our Xenon purpose statement focused on additional forms of entertainment, ultimately including music, TV, movies, and every shade of entertainment in between. The clear goal was to attract new customers by expanding on our beachhead with gamers. To do this, we built on our most significant differentiator, the Xbox Live service, which was already wildly exceeding our high expectations on the original Xbox. Our goal was to turn Xbox Live into a diverse entertainment service that a broad demographic would value and enjoy.

Even in gaming, we knew we had to produce experiences that appealed to a wider audience. Our research showed that some parents, and especially mothers, would not allow an Xbox into the living room or even into the house. For that reason, our Xenon purpose statement emphasized innovation in entertainment and implied that we wanted a wider variety of games, including games that some called "casual games" or "games for kids." This represented a real cultural shift for the team, especially those working on the creative side, but it was an essential element in achieving scale and ultimate success.

As things would play out, Nintendo did us one better in this arena with their innovative motion controller for the Wii, a product designed and priced to sell to a mass audience. Although not envisioned in our original Xenon work, our eventual development of the Kinect sensor was an effort to continue broadening the audience by eliminating the need to be skillful with a gaming controller. The Kinect enabled players to use body motion and voice to control the game going beyond the Wii-mote's use of a hand wand. It also was an excellent response to the first-mover advantage enjoyed by Nintendo with the Wii.

Although the words seem simple and perhaps non-descript, the purpose statement in the three-page document was a solid foundation for the rest of the Xenon strategy work. It effectively communicated important, fundamental changes in our approach and empowered the team to make corresponding changes in each of their specific groups, moving the strategy process a level deeper in the organization. The marketing team translated the purpose statement into the tagline "Your Games, Your Friends, Your Lifestyle," a big step away from the original Xbox tagline "There's No Power Greater Than X."

YES, VIRGINIA, PRINCIPLES DO MATTER

With the purpose statement for Xenon in place, the next challenge in building our strategic house was to identify the second P of our 3P Framework—principles. I've always thought of myself as a principled person, someone you could trust to do the right thing. Although I think that is true at a personal level, one of my professional failures during the development of the original Xbox was an inability, and perhaps unwillingness, to establish guidelines by which everyone in the group would live and operate. My timeout for reflection shone a light on that failing, and in implementing our new approach to strategy, I didn't make that mistake again. Like the *New York Sun's* response to Virginia O'Hanlon, the girl

> I am here to report that principles absolutely do matter. Without them, a team has no central rudder to keep it on course.

who asked, "Is there a Santa Claus?" I am here to report that principles absolutely do matter. Without them, a team has no central rudder to keep it on course.

Controlling the rudder that keeps an organization on track is much like navigating a ship at sea. Imagine being Christopher Columbus sailing off into the horizon with no weather forecast, no map, and three really small ships. Your tools are a sextant and a compass, your own experience, and no small amount of courage. If you translate that to a modern business or civic organization, you now have many more tools, ranging from spreadsheets to sophisticated modeling programs with "big data" as the new frontier for understanding your position in the marketplace. But much of the real navigation happens within the culture of the organization, and that requires a different set of tools, much like the compasses and sextants of old. I call these tools principles.

Creating the principles that will guide an organization is an incredibly important step, though it is one that most leaders allow to happen through osmosis rather than thoughtful selection. Often by the time they decide to be explicit, they over-architect this portion of the strategy and create a laundry list of things that are "good to do." Setting a limit of five principles and communicating them consistently across the company, both in formal and informal ways, is very important to establishing a lasting strategic framework.

The 2002 edition of the Microsoft Executive Staff Retreat—the same annual retreat that initiated the Xbox odyssey in 1999—turned into a referendum on the appropriateness of the company's culture and whether we were focused on delivering value to our customers in the right way. This discussion took place in the wake of a long, drawn-out Microsoft antitrust case in the US and Europe. As a result of this tumultuous retreat, the senior leadership team was very responsive to the issues raised and made real efforts to define and communicate cultural attributes across the company. But in true Microsoft fashion, we over-analyzed and over-intellectualized the process defining six values and seven tenets that described the culture of the company and the attributes we were looking for in employees. I don't know many people who could remember that many values and tenets much less live up to them.

Other organizations address this challenge with more positive outcomes. As part of my Xbox experience, I spent significant time with retailers around the world. Larger retailers like Walmart and Costco employ hundreds of thousands of employees in many countries, so they have to be especially good at establishing core concepts that everyone can apply consistently. Although I've never discussed the 3P Framework with anyone at any of these companies, it's fairly easy to interpolate their essential principles.

All you have to do to understand the core principles at Walmart is to spend some time with any of their merchants. They will all tell you, "We will deliver the lowest prices in the market, guaranteed." The executives I worked with at Walmart lived this principle every day, demanding the best terms and conditions from suppliers and controlling their own expenses. I went to dinner one year with Walmart executives at the Consumer Electronics Show in Las Vegas and was not allowed to pay for their dinner—that would have violated a clear company principle to ensure they were not unduly influenced by their suppliers. After dinner, those of us on the Microsoft team jumped into a couple of hired town cars to return to our hotel, something that was common during CES when getting a taxi was often very difficult. On the way, we saw the Walmart execs walking the half mile back to their hotel, where they told us they were sharing rooms. This was living proof that every Walmart employee, on every level of the organization, bought into the core cost-saving principle.

As a club store for members only, Costco has a very different business model from Walmart and other retailers. In meetings, they will say, "Our members are special, so we only sell products that offer something unique to our membership." Consequently, our relationship with Costco involved special packaging, product bundles, and merchandising requirements. For instance, the Xbox team planned a yearly holiday promotion to drive traffic and sales during November and December. A few of the specifics varied by retailer, but the basic promotional offer was the same—except at the membership warehouses like Costco. To maintain our position on the sales floor, we had to put together different offerings packaged together in a unique way to Costco specifications, quantities, and timelines. We had to adhere to their core "our-members-are-special" principle.

MAKING A PRINCIPLED STATEMENT

I have no way of knowing how difficult it was for these companies to define their principles, but at Microsoft, the Xbox team struggled to find a comparable cultural compass. In large part, this issue was caused by the team's composition: a collection of people from many different backgrounds and multiple perspectives. Melting pots can produce some amazing outcomes, but the process is not always pretty, and as a leader, sometimes you don't want to know what is going on in the sausage factory.

The Xbox team felt the need to prove it belonged in the hardcore gaming world, and this insecurity manifested itself in every area, including the parties held for the industry, the marketing materials created, and the content produced. The team went to extremes to attract attention, and not always the kind of attention some of us had in mind. While outrageousness was not a new phenomenon in the gaming space, Xbox achieved a new level of "out of the box" with an ad produced for the launch in the UK. Picture a woman giving birth and launching her baby through a window. The baby flies through the air, and the figure ages until it is very old, at which point it lands in a coffin in a graveyard. The tagline appears on the screen: "Life is Short, Play More." The ad was arresting—on so many levels.

On the game content side, we found our footing a bit more quickly. Many Microsoft employees were uncomfortable with the nature of some game content, in particular around violence and sexual themes, and were worried about the impact on the Microsoft brand. In response, we established a set of principles around content. Every game had to be rated by an independent group, and we were the first to include parental controls on a console. At the same time, one of our principles defended game creators' rights to freedom of expression, declaring that games were covered under the First Amendment. Although all of this caused considerable controversy within the team because it ran counter to the desire to prove our "gaming manhood," these efforts to empower parents and at the same time support creative expression struck the right chord with the market. Gamers realized that the system had no downside for them, and parents liked the concept of having controls, even if many did not use them.

By the time we got to the offsite at the Salish Lodge, it was abundantly clear that we needed to internalize the importance of principles and communicate them effectively to the team. We were still not thinking of this in a formal 3P Framework context, but the Xenon three-pager articulated operating and cultural guidelines along the following lines:

- **_Maximize Return to Investors:_** For all of its success in gaining market share, Xbox lost five to seven billion dollars during its four-year life, certainly some sort of dubious record in any business and definitely an "investment" leader in the video game space. With Xenon, we were crystal clear that the business had to make money—not just a few hundred million dollars but in the billions-of-dollars range. This change in approach required a significant end-to-end redesign across all aspects of the business, including everything from maximizing the attach rate of Xbox Live subscribers to redesigning our packaging to reduce shipping costs.

- **_Reach New Customers and Expand the Market:_** In addition to transforming the profitability of our products, we also needed significantly more volume to cover the substantial fixed costs in development and marketing associated with a console launch. We pushed the team to grow the market, believing we would have a better chance to win over newer, less committed customers rather than trying to take share from Sony. With video games in only 40 percent of US households at the time and far fewer outside the US, this seemed like a good bet.

- ***Optimize for Gaming First, Then Digital Lifestyle:*** We decided to secure our core gaming customers first and then expand into other forms of digital entertainment. Exploring new types of games beyond sports, speed, explosions, fantasy, and guns required some careful planning because we didn't have the creative talent or proper culture for these new types of games. We directed the team to secure this part of the plan before pursuing a broader media initiative around what came to be known as the "digital lifestyle."

- ***Build a Global Business:*** I often express pride in how quickly we spread the Xbox business around the world, but the truth is the original Xbox was for English speakers. The team's perspective was very US-centric and our major differentiator, Xbox Live, emphasized social interaction with voice. Both of these characteristics biased our business toward markets similar to the US and/or where English was spoken. With Xenon, we absolutely needed to be successful in more markets, and to do that, every aspect of the plan had to address local conditions across some forty countries.

- ***Think Better Together:*** As much as I loved the people in the United Nations of Xbox, Xenon's success required a fully integrated team.

We had to knit the software and hardware together in a more thoughtful, orchestrated way, and our internal game developers had to understand the features that differentiated the system and take advantage of them in their games. Furthermore, going up against Sony, we had to broaden this concept of working together beyond the Xbox group to include many other Microsoft assets.

Articulating these principles helped mold our merry band of gamers into a more cohesive unit—an important milestone in the project. Of course, this did not happen overnight, nor was it without its trials and tribulations. We had to continue to fight the team's desire to optimize locally rather than for the overall business, and some very talented and respected people ended up leaving the group because they disagreed with this approach. While losing these key individuals was stressful for the team and personally very painful, it was necessary to the unification of the team and the validation of the strategy. Sometimes there is such a thing as addition through subtraction. The difficult part for me was determining when to fight to keep someone and when to allow or encourage them to move on. Being dispassionate about this was not easy, hence the need for principles, but the best leaders know painful changes in the short term are often beneficial for both the team and the individuals involved over the long run.

XBOX LIVE: A CASE STUDY

The development of Xbox Live is a canonical example of principles driving product creation. Early in the Xbox project, we concluded that playing console video games online was a significant opportunity, one that we needed to exploit to compete successfully with Sony and

Nintendo. Recognizing its importance was not the same as agreeing to a plan, and we had long arguments about how to formulate that strategy from a product and from a business perspective. Our poor decision-making framework delayed the development of an online plan and ultimately meant that Xbox Live launched a full year after the original product.

Although the 3P Framework approach was still a long way off, J Allard and his team placed a heavy emphasis on establishing core principles as they moved Xbox Live out of the conceptual stage and into product development. In fact, one of the secrets to our ultimate success in the online world was the early establishment of five principles for Xbox Live:

1. ***Voice in Every Game:*** We required every game developed for Xbox Live to support voice communications. At the time, this was viewed by many as a crazy requirement. Some were concerned that voice would be difficult to implement technically, others worried the quality of the experience would be poor, and still others just did not understand the value. We addressed these concerns with some significant development work to make voice relatively easy to include technically and to ensure that the gamer experience was consistently up to standards. This single feature became a key part of creating a social gaming community almost a year before MySpace was launched, and long before Facebook or Twitter established social networking as a new medium.

2. ***Persistent ID:*** When customers joined Xbox Live, they created a user name called a Gamer Tag that became their persona whenever they were on the service. We required each game, regardless

of publisher, to support the Xbox Live Gamer Tag system so that players would have the same name in every game. This enabled a gamer to build a persona, reputation, and record of achievement across the service. From their perspective, this was both logical and convenient because they only had to create a name once and manage one password across all of their Xbox games. That notwithstanding, our publishing partners wanted to have a unique ID for each customer within their set of games—something we did not allow.

3. ***Unified Friends List:*** As players met others on the network, Xbox Live enabled them to create a friends list, which they shared across all games on the service. We required every publisher to support this list in their games. This definitely fostered the community that was so important to the future of Xbox Live, and it enabled people to find each other regardless of which game they wanted to play. Again, publishers wanted players to have game-specific friends lists rather than sharing the network effect of social interactivity across games from other publishers. Today this concept is taken for granted, thanks to the role it plays in services like Facebook and Twitter, but in 2001, this was a relatively novel and controversial approach.

4. ***Secure Gaming Experience:*** Online gaming was still a wild, wild, west experience in 2001, and Xbox Live needed to be substantially better. In response, we developed a team mantra: "No hackers, no sharks, no hassles." This might seem like an obvious thing to do, but it created backlash with our partners because it required every gamer to log in to Microsoft's servers. They viewed this as

an encroachment on their customer base and believed it would enable Microsoft to steal their consumers and collect data on their gaming habits. In our minds, security was a mutual interest, and the Xbox Live team agreed to share any data that was appropriate to gather. As publishers began to understand the privacy issues and the scope of the technical challenges, they became more accepting of this approach.

5. ***Subscription Service:*** From the start, Xbox Live committed to a business model that required customers to pay a subscription ($49 per year at the time) in order to play games against others. Eventually, other services, like Netflix, were included in this subscription to create even more value. Nearly 100 percent of the people pre-briefed on Xbox Live said the subscription fee was a mistake. They said gamers would never pay for online gaming and the service should be offered for free, at least at the outset. Publishing partners complained that charging a subscription enabled Microsoft to generate revenue from their content. The view from Xbox land was that customers would be willing to pay for a great experience and offering it for free would create an expectation that would be difficult to change in the future. In terms of economics, this was an incredibly important decision, generating hundreds of millions of dollars in profits for the Xbox business and its partners.

These five principles guided the decisions of every group involved in creating Xbox Live. Without them, we could easily have wavered, conceded, and floundered. The principles provided courage to make the hard choices that enabled us to take the lead in the console online gaming world.

Our strongest competitor, Sony, took a completely different approach. In the PS2 era, online gaming was never a central part of their product roadmap despite frequent promotional announcements and proclamations about their commitment to networked computing. While they did offer online games on their system, which they touted as a free service, the experience varied widely from game to game, with none of the consistency, convenience, or community found on Xbox Live. Their network was not reliable, in part because they allowed individual publishers to create their own services and they had numerous security issues. For its part, Nintendo basically ignored online gaming during the GameCube era and, even in the subsequent Wii generation, did a very poor job of creating the infrastructure for a successful service.

The rousing success of Xbox Live continues today with over forty million subscribers on the service—a number that is several multiples higher than our original projections. Despite all of the concerns and issues expressed, the Xbox Live approach triumphed for three reasons. First, the team was deeply committed to its principles, to the point of creating a major public rift with Electronic Arts, who disagreed on a number of important online concepts. Mending this part of the EA relationship required two years of careful planning and negotiation to allow both entities to live within their individual sets of principles.

Second, we focused on creating an awesome customer experience, one that ensured that Xbox Live delivered the best social gaming environment on the market and the premier place for people to gather. We designed Xbox Live to be the Disney World of online gaming, and everything else was just the county fair. Down the road, the loyalty of Xbox Live players created a customer base that stayed with Xbox even as the platform moved from Xbox to Xbox 360.

Third, Xbox Live generated significant revenue and profits which the team reinvested in the platform and service to make it even better for customers and more challenging for competitors to match. Largely because of this foundation and continued innovation, Xbox Live is by far the most important element in the Xbox success story and drives a significant portion of the platform's customer engagement and profitable economics.

Building Xbox Live was my first real education in the power of principles—and with appreciation to J Allard and many others, it's a lesson I've never forgotten. Together with the work done to establish a clear purpose, this new-found focus on principles laid a solid foundation for Xenon, and the three-pager was two-thirds complete. The last phase of the process, establishing priorities, was the most difficult because it required choices to be made, projects to be approved, and pet projects to be sacrificed. Saying no is never easy, and Xenon proved to be no exception.

THE NOBLE ART OF
LEAVING THINGS UNDONE

Articulating our Xenon purpose and principles was a big step in the right direction for the team, as it would be for any organization—business, nonprofit, or civic. These foundational elements helped the XLT unify its operating approach and initiate the building of a specific Xbox culture. The impact was not immediate or dramatic, but over time, the team's effectiveness improved markedly. Beyond reshaping the organization, purpose and principles also played a major role in setting our priorities—the third P in the 3P Framework.

Setting priorities requires a team to turn its attention to specific areas for action and investment. In most organizations, the challenge is not deciding which things should be on the laundry list of activities; usually the problem is determining what *not* to do, concentrating resources and energies on the areas that have greatest impact. To paraphrase Chinese author Lin Yutang, it is best to leave some things undone.

> In most organizations, the challenge is not deciding which things should be on the laundry list of activities; usually the problem is determining what not to do, concentrating resources and energies on the areas that have greatest impact.

The Rule of 3s and 5s comes into play once again here, demanding a limit of five key priorities in a strategic plan, whether it's an overarching plan for an entire company or governmental entity or a strategy for a particular product or civic initiative. This level of focus is a difficult and challenging task for even the most disciplined organizations, and resistance will come from many directions at once.

Some people will turn this into a "tyranny-of-or" process by putting something on the cut list they know is important to the organization or its leader in order to expand the list of priorities. Another common ploy is to pit two important items against each other, forcing either a tradeoff or expansion of the list. Leaders need to resist this type of organizational inertia and force people to make real, productive choices. They also need to recognize (and be rest assured) that the priority list does not exclude other work. As long as the key initiatives receive the required focus, the team can and certainly will complete many, more specific tasks that are not on the priority list. If the top five priorities are addressed effectively, this is a totally acceptable and desirable outcome.

TOOLS OF THE TRADE

Setting priorities is a simple idea, but selecting the right priorities is complicated, and it can't be done in a vacuum. These initiatives are the ultimate proof points for the strategy and must reflect all of the information available to the team, including the market expertise, knowledge, and intuition of those with more experience. In addition, there are many other tools beyond purpose and principles that can and should be used to provide insight and facilitate the tradeoffs necessary in the decision-making process. Ignore any one of these additional data points at your peril.

Nothing in the 3P Framework diminishes the value that a SWOT analysis, a Boston Consulting Group growth-share matrix, Porter's

5 Forces Competitive Model, or a strategic simulation can generate. Without going into the specifics of each of these techniques, their purpose is to force a holistic approach to strategy development, enabling the team to step back from the specific issues of day-to-day operations to see the broader forest of challenges they face. We used several of these tools in our Xbox work and found them invaluable. In some ways, the 3P Framework gathers the results garnered from using these techniques and integrates them into a clear, cohesive strategic plan that can be communicated and implemented effectively.

Since many of these approaches are all well documented, I will focus on a tool used by a friend and former Microsoft colleague, Brad Chase, in his consulting practice. He calls this approach "Double-Down Bets" because it forces companies to identify key differentiators that can drive dramatic value in their business and invest in them aggressively. Brad challenges organizations to identify transformative products or services that have what he refers to as "eye-popping" customer value. At the same time, he urges them to find profitable and if possible, game-changing, business models that appeal to a broad range of customers in order to monetize the eye-popping value.

Apple exhibited this behavior to great effect with the introduction of the iPod and iTunes. On the customer-value side of the equation, their system was remarkably easy and elegant to use, creating a truly smile-inducing customer experience. They leveraged this design and ease of use to shift the industry's business model from software profits to making money on the devices themselves. What's more, they enhanced their business model with a new, ninety-nine-cent, single-song track offer that provided better value to their customers. To cap it all off, they disaggregated the music publishers and labels, effectively taking most of the profits in the non-performance portion of the industry. That is a successful Double-Down Bet.

THE XENON FIVE

In many respects, the original Xbox work was a rehearsal and training ground for developing a strong set of priorities for Xenon. The team gained valuable market experience, learned a number of difficult and expensive lessons, and developed its own sense of what mattered to our partners and customers. This on-the-job training was especially important for me as CXO since I had no particular background or sensibilities about the video game market. We also utilized a number of traditional strategy tools to stress-test our new-found intuition about Xenon's path to success.

In 3P Framework terms, we incorporated all of this intelligence into five key priorities for the Xenon three-pager. Selecting these initiatives was definitely the most contentious part of our strategy framework development because it forced the XLT to make concrete, lasting decisions. After much debate and discussion, we established and communicated the following priorities in the original April 2003 document (with some confidential information redacted and technical jargon eliminated):

1. ***Exclusive Entertainment Content and Services:*** This is the highest priority because it is the lifeblood of the Xbox business. We must build a plan that utilizes Microsoft-owned franchises like Halo, some targeted games published by others like Call of Duty, and our Xbox Live services, all of which contribute to ensuring that Xenon is the best interactive entertainment platform. Our content plan must describe how we are going to utilize our key game

franchises (timing, product concept, etc.), what requirements the Microsoft studios have to execute the plan, and how the platform, content, and services teams are going to work together to achieve this result. We have to do this for all of the major world markets, especially for Japan. For those titles that are going to be on both Xenon and PlayStation3 (PS3), we need to provide the right tools and ecosystem dynamics that maximize the likelihood that these titles ship at the same time on both consoles. In the ideal scenario, these titles would start as Xenon titles and migrate later to PS3.

2. ***Customer Value and Differentiation:*** Sony is an entrenched, established leader with 60 to 70 percent share of current-generation console sales around the world. While we should be proud of our 20 to 25 percent share in North America and Europe, we have a long way to go to reach our installed-base goals. Ensuring that Xenon is a clearly differentiated product that provides great customer value is critical to this effort. Differentiation starts with a clear definition of our target audience, their needs, and the experiences that excite them. Differentiation without this first step runs the risk of merely being "different." Ultimately, we need value propositions that clearly state why Xenon is more valuable for each of the following target audiences: consumers, publishers, game developers, retailers, suppliers, and our internal Microsoft partners. Put differently, it is critical that we shift our value proposition away from "speeds-and-feeds performance" and focus on customer experiences (content and services). Given that we are competing with Sony, it is especially important that we do a great job evolving and developing the Xbox brand to have strong, positive meaning for our target audiences.

3. **Profit:** Many of the tradeoffs we need to make in building the Xenon plan revolve around how much we can or want to spend acquiring customers versus returning profit to the company. I want to be clear about how we should think about this. We need to reach our critical mass sales goal, which I will define as a worldwide market share of 40 percent. Along with achieving this objective, we will optimize all of our activities around making money for Microsoft. Our goal should be for the console hardware to break even or make a small profit over the Xenon life cycle. Across the consolidated P&L (which adds Microsoft games, games from publishers, Xbox Live, sales and marketing costs, and all of our overhead), I'm challenging the team to design a business model that makes [redacted] in profit during the Xenon cycle. Profits on game content, both from Microsoft and from fees paid to us by other publishers will make up the majority of this return. This will be supplemented by profit on peripheral products like game controllers, which were unprofitable on Xbox 1. Finally, Xbox Live must be an important source of profits targeting a [redacted] percent subscription attach rate to each console sold and [redacted] percent of the profit target. Making all of this happen will require significant changes and process improvements across all aspects of our business practices. As one example, we should design a product and business model that can last eight to ten years rather than the four- to five-year Xbox 1 life cycle.

4. **Time to Market:** We have been saying externally and internally that we would ship Xenon whenever Sony ships PS3, but we need to change this timing and approach for the internal team. If we want

to gain share on Sony, we have to ship the base Xenon product by Fall/Holiday 2005 in all major regions (North America, Europe, Japan), and we have to make this mandatory for the team. From a competitive perspective, we must be ready to launch at the same time they do, assuming they are on a Holiday 2005 plan. My view is that if they believe we are going in Holiday 2005, they won't be willing to risk waiting. In any event, we *must* have a differentiated offering regardless of timing, and we have the financial commitment to drive hard against Sony if they decide to wait. In terms of territory and feature tradeoffs, there is no requirement to ship every market on the exact same day. In fact, the plan of record should reflect a staggered launch beginning in North America, moving to Europe, and finishing in Japan (where holiday happens later). This maximizes our ability to generate momentum through early success in our stronger markets and to build on that success in Japan. At this stage of the project, it is difficult to speculate which features we would cut or delay to hit this date, but suffice it to say this date is a major requirement and we will consider feature cuts before we slip the console date.

5. *The Fifteen-Month Campaign:* One lesson we've learned from Xbox 1 is that "the launch" is only the first step toward establishing success. With hardware supply constraints and an enthusiast audience, the laws of supply and demand encourage early positive results. But sustaining a strong start all the way through the second holiday is very challenging: the audience broadens, consoles from all competitors are in good supply, pricing and other promotional efforts play a stronger role, and content breadth and depth become even more important. Therefore, to win with Xenon, we need an

integrated plan that is established well in advance to run a fifteen-month campaign that drives success from fall 2005 through December 2006. Creating this "wave effect" means developing conscious strategies for our content and services roadmaps (down to the geography/studio/franchise/brand level) to maximize console sales. It also implies strong integration in our plans for cost reductions (which increase pricing flexibility), marketing, and sales efforts to drive share effectively. All of this is especially important if Sony decides to wait until fall 2006 to ship PS3. In that case, we will need to execute very, very well to combat their pre-launch activities.

In many respects, these priorities grew out of the Xenon principles, in particular the connection between shareholder return and profit and the global nature of the business. The Fifteen-Month Campaign concept was also tremendously significant. The team morphed this into the First Two Holiday Campaign, or in Microsoft jargon, FTHC, and in the process changed the way they thought about almost every aspect of our plan—from first principles to beyond the launch period. Each group had to continue their work on the original Xbox, execute on the plan to sunset that product, and plan for the launch of Xenon and the Holiday 2006 work—all at the same time. While this put tremendous stress on the organization and required equal parts planning and endurance, it was critical to the success of the product we ultimately called Xbox 360.

With the benefit of hindsight, there are aspects of this framework I would have changed. In our desire to beat Sony, for instance, we left our flank exposed to Nintendo's push toward the casual gaming audience, and we didn't think through the process of extending the

Xbox 360 life cycle beyond five years. Responses to these issues and other challenges we faced had to be developed in real time, which is never optimal for any team.

With those caveats, actual events played out in a way that fit this strategy remarkably well, or perhaps the strategy influenced how things played out. When Sony decided to wait until Holiday 2006 to launch PS3, having the FTHC plan in place was both prescient and fortuitous. Xbox was able to capitalize on the opening when Sony announced very high launch prices and produced a product that was difficult for developers to utilize. Looking back on it, I'm impressed by the team's fidelity to the plan. They executed these initiatives consistently and at a high level of quality well through the Xbox 360 product cycle. Thanks to the strategic process and a number of missteps by our competitors, the outcome was a success well beyond our original plan, both in market share and profit.

There is something satisfying about thinking through a problem and crafting five simple approaches to addressing those issues, but publishing the Xenon three-pager was not a seminal event within Microsoft. It was just another memo from a group trying to organize itself to create the second version of a marginally successful first-generation product. In reality, however, the 3P Framework process was a major breakthrough—communicating the strategy across the team and up the Microsoft executive chain enabled better decision making and saved us from many strategic debates later on. It put a framework in place within which other elements could be finalized and unleashed the creative and operational strengths of what was quickly becoming a very skilled team.

THE XENON CUTTING ROOM FLOOR

The Rule of 3s and 5s provides focus that is critical from a resource allocation, as well as a communications perspective, especially for any complex set of problems. None of the challenges facing Xenon were easy issues, and as the events following 9/11 demonstrate, the civic issues we face are logarithmically more complex than those faced in the video game space. Radical focus enables you to bring the right tools to bear on a problem and communicate an overall strategy that people can understand. Without it, no real change is possible.

> Radical focus enables you to bring the right tools to bear on a problem and communicate an overall strategy that people can understand. Without it, no real change is possible.

When I discuss this level of focus, I hear statements like, "At my company, clearly more than five things are getting done at any one time," or "Some of my employees are doing essential tasks that are not directly related to the five priorities." Establishing priorities ensures that the five most important things get done effectively and prevents other issues from creating confusion or getting in the way. With that said, the proverbial trains need to keep running and everyday functions that are a part of the heartbeat of an organization must continue even if they are not highlighted in the five priorities. The task at hand is to establish and resource the strategic priorities, enable the organization to keep running, and eliminate any initiatives that are not critical to long-term success.

During the Xenon experience, the team considered a number of activities beyond the five priorities we ultimately established. Some of these tasks were clearly day-to-day tactical work that would continue as part of the regular operations of the group. Other initiatives we evaluated were ultimately off strategy and risked distracting the team. As the group's leader, I would love to report I managed a really disciplined process and making these choices was easy or straightforward. In fact, we ran down some lonely, dusty trails and found more than a few empty rabbit holes before we re-centered ourselves based on the concepts in the 3P Framework. Keeping several thousand people

In fact, we ran down some lonely, dusty trails and found more than a few empty rabbit holes before we re-centered ourselves based on the concepts in the 3P Framework.

on the straight and narrow path was not easy. Sometimes we got it right, and in other cases, we wandered off strategy and had to learn from mistakes:

- *Run the Xbox Business (for a while):* As mentioned above, the entire Xenon project was conceived, planned, and executed while we were still building, marketing, and selling the original Xbox. In the face of significant financial loses, product sales and market share were still very important in terms of building engagement with consumers and supporting Xbox's publishing partners, who were making reasonably good money selling games. This was especially true as the strength of the Xbox Live asset became clear, and acquiring Xbox Live customers became an important element to support the Xenon launch.

  Of course, this created real stress for the team as people had to make tradeoffs between devoting time to the current Xbox business and the future Xenon work. In some cases, the team was expanded, but in most cases people had to broaden their roles appropriately. Eventually, it became clear we could not continue the Xbox business, in particular given its absolutely ugly financial profile and the way it distracted us from our five Xenon priorities. While Sony would continue their PS2 business for some time after PS3 shipped (after all, they were making money on it), we stopped manufacturing Xboxes and removed the product from the market just as Xbox 360 was shipping. While more of an overlap would have been helpful, we stuck true to the Xenon priorities and focused exclusively on Xbox 360 sooner than our partners would have liked.

- *Build the Xboy:* Several groups made presentations to the XLT arguing that we should pursue a handheld product that would be complementary to Xbox and compete with Nintendo's GameBoy and Sony's PlayStation Portable (PSP). The basic idea behind these "Xboy" proposals was that Microsoft needed a complete product line to capture a younger audience, gain more retail shelf space, and provide opportunities for publishers to leverage their Xbox investments. In theory, there was money to be made in this market, but as with Xbox, investment would be required first.

  Each time this came up, we decided it would be a distraction, require an entirely new team to execute, and provide minimal leverage in the overall console battle. We had to get Xbox right before considering other product lines. The advent of smartphones ultimately created real problems for Nintendo and Sony in their handheld markets. Staying true to the priorities saved us from a significant strategic and financial mistake and enabled us to stay focused on a successful Xenon launch.

- *Expand into New Markets:* Microsoft had official subsidiaries in over seventy countries and business interests in many more.

Consequently, there were always country managers asking the team to bring Xbox to their market. International growth was also enticing because it enabled us to enter territories where we could establish an early advantage—or at least not be as far behind as we were in the US, Europe, and Japan. In some cases, like China, this was a difficult challenge because of government restrictions and business model issues, and despite meaningful resources expended, we never did ship Xbox or Xbox 360 into mainland China.

Entering other markets appeared to be more straightforward, requiring some safety testing, a distributor relationship, and perhaps a bit of language localization. But in most cases, it was a mistake to succumb to internal pressure and over-commit to more countries. India, a market with little gaming background but a growing consumer class, is a perfect example. The local subsidiary convinced us to launch Xbox there, but government regulations and tariffs drove up the console price, distribution was difficult, and Indian cultural tastes proved to be different from the rest of the world. Thousands of very expensive units sat on retail and warehouse shelves gathering dust. Wanting to be global was one of our core principles, but chasing low volumes for the wrong reasons distracted the team. There is no such thing as a free lunch, and we tried to eat at the global buffet a bit too often.

The Xenon three-pager, along with considerable analysis, enabled us to make these types of tradeoffs, more often than not leading to a "no" decision. Of course, these decisions on potential projects aren't necessarily permanent, as conditions change frequently. Strategic priorities should be reviewed at regular intervals, somewhere between six months and two years depending on the business and market circumstances. It is perfectly acceptable to say "no" to something for now and return to the topic as other priorities are either completed or become less relevant. This process keeps the strategy up to date while providing the flexibility to respond to changes in the marketplace or the needs of the organization.

THE GAMIFICATION TEST

Applying gaming principles and development processes to real-world problems is a hot trend. You see this in everything from education and training to marketing and promotional efforts. "Levels, power-ups, rewards, and boss opponents" are concepts being applied to a variety of problems, and we used this gamification approach as a "tools of the trade" test of our strategic framework.

With the five core Xenon priorities defined, the planning team decided to do some game-theory work as part of a rigorous process to verify assumptions, validate concepts, and consider alternatives. During this phase, we conducted a formal market simulation, focusing on our competition with Sony. We hired a consulting firm to construct a two-day, role-playing exercise in which team members personified Microsoft, Sony, retailers, developers, and publishers. The goal of the exercise was to explore various market scenarios and understand how our plan would fare against the moves we assumed Sony would make.

I'm generally not a great fan of consulting firms, in part because their typical process involves interviewing everyone in your organization to extract knowledge that they then organize and report back to you. In my view, this isn't a value-added exercise. In fairness, I also have a stubborn streak, and requesting outside help somehow feels like a failure. My pride notwithstanding, in this case we needed the additional expertise to construct an independently developed mechanism that reflected market reality and drove us to a measurable conclusion. The consultants created an interesting and effective process that led to a very interactive two-day retreat where we played out the simulation and then analyzed the results.

We held the simulation at a local hotel, which at various times has been a Red Lion, a Doubletree, and a Hilton—I believe this was still in the Doubletree phase, but the venue has not really changed in twenty years. On the main floor behind the breakfast restaurant, there is a large, ill-shaped room that is used for meetings and private functions. The décor is straight out of the late 1970s and generally makes you wonder who would have a "special event" in the room, all of which was perfect for our band of amateur actors rehearsing for their debut in the video game wars movie.

Roughly thirty of us divided into role-playing teams—Sony, game publishers, game developers, Microsoft, and others. Following the rules of the game, each group made economic decisions based on the information presented to them and the actions of other groups. Over two days, we ran through a few different scenarios to understand how each one would affect market share and profit. The team really enjoyed the game, in part because it gave them the chance to personify various players in the industry. Their caricatures were at once laughable and valuable, and beyond the simulation results, the role-playing turned into a great team-bonding exercise.

The consistent winner in the process was not Sony or Microsoft but the publishers like Electronic Arts and Activision. This outcome is not really surprising when you consider the adage "content is king." Microsoft and Sony certainly created their own games, but both were highly dependent on others for key franchises and new product concepts. As someone who had to partner and negotiate with publishers every day, I was glad they didn't witness these results that demonstrated how much power they actually had in the market.

This gamification experiment changed our plan in important ways, including acknowledging that publisher content was critical to our success and justifying increased resources for those relationships. Even though it was very late in the development process, we also made key modifications to our product specifications, doubling the size of our system memory. This change was part of our effort to woo publishers and developers and although expensive, played a critical role in our ability to compete with Sony in game quality.

The Sony simulation enabled the team to take a proactive approach to planning, but that doesn't mean we didn't learn some hard lessons from real life. In all of our work, we were exclusively concerned with Sony as our major competitor, effectively ignoring the possible actions of Nintendo. While this laser focus was helpful in many ways and a huge reason for the market success of Xbox 360, we left ourselves exposed to Nintendo's next-generation plans, an issue that hit me right between the eyes at their presentation at the Tokyo Game Show in September 2005. Nintendo CEO Satoru Iwata showed an innovative motion controller called the Wii Remote in action for the first time, and it was very impressive. I was sitting in the first row at the presentation and vividly remember thinking, *Yikes. I hope someone on the team can explain to me why this isn't a problem.* Hoping something will go away has never been a great approach to a competitive situation.

> I was sitting in the first row at the presentation and vividly remember thinking, *Yikes. I hope someone on the team can explain to me why this isn't a problem.* Hoping something will go away has never been a great approach to a competitive situation.

Nintendo shipped the Wii game console in 2006, and while it was relatively low-powered—it did not even support high-definition graphics—the ease of use and intuitiveness of the Wii Remote and a $249 price point vaulted it to the front of the console class. For the first two years of the next generation, the Wii outsold Xbox 360 and PS3 by meaningful margins in most markets. This Nintendo "surprise" was an important lesson in challenging assumptions in the priority-setting process.

Eventually, the Wii's lack of power, weak online gaming, and poor non-gaming capabilities caught up with it, and both Xbox 360 and PS3 passed it in market share. Xbox 360 surged into the lead and during the course of that generation sold 80M consoles, far outstripping our original targets in the three-pager. Some of this success was a natural outcome of excellent execution work by a team hitting its stride, but all of that great work was grounded in a robust, common-sense strategy. The Xenon team used its early version of the 3P Framework to develop a clear, simple purpose, rally the team around concrete principles, and focus its resources on five key priorities. Fleshing out the details in the thirty-page phase of the 3/30/300 paradigm remained as a final chasm to be crossed.

6

THE END OF THE BEGINNING

We all learn in geometry that the shortest distance between two points is a straight line. The 3P Framework and its common-sense approach to planning provided the XLT with a great foundation and a clear vision for our ultimate goal. Navigating the gap between those two points, however, was anything but a straight line. With our three-page plan complete (see Appendix A for the Xenon three-pager), the team realized that we weren't quite at the end of the beginning and there would be many zigs and zags before we were done. Indeed, we moved directly from arguments over priorities to the massive challenge of building more detailed plans within each initiative.

Logic dictated that J Allard, the chief product visionary, should handle this next step, which would expand on the three-page framework and provide more specific direction in the thirty-page phase of the process. The fallacy in this approach revealed itself immediately, as the level of detail required in a thirty-page plan exceeded any one individual's ability to grasp all of the specifics. The plan had to cover areas of the strategy tangentially related to J's areas of expertise, making his authorship of the thirty-pager even more difficult. After one aborted draft, we quickly shifted gears to a group-driven approach, involving experts from each function within the team.

After a few more false starts, we created the Xenon Integration Group (the "XIG" in Microsoft acronym-speak), comprising fifteen team members charged with drafting a thirty-pager that inevitably ballooned to over eighty PowerPoint slides. This slide deck went through the Xenon strategy from top to bottom and proposed the core elements required in each part of the business to fulfill our three-page ambitions. The full leadership team then reviewed and debated the final proposal, including a final two-day marathon, validating and integrating elements of the plan.

There was a great deal of wrangling at the outset over who would lead the XIG, as my direct reports and the XIG participants themselves perceived this as important. We tried a number of different configurations, most of which led to people coming to my office complaining about biased or misguided leadership. While some of this was certainly about ego and perceived status within the organization, people raised legitimate questions about skill set, blind spots, and interpersonal capabilities. After all, this was a very important decision that would establish organizational power and some level of control over the future of Xenon. This was a make-or-break decision for me, because like many CEOs, I found it was one of the few ways I could directly affect the success of a specific program.

Ultimately, I picked the head of our hardware team, Todd Holmdahl, to run the XIG. In part I chose him for the central role he played in the project, but more importantly because of his credibility with the rest of the team. Todd, in many ways, was the textbook definition of the self-less leader, and while people sometimes disagreed with him or wished he had some specific skill that they thought was important, they always respected him. Todd was battle tested by the original Xbox launch and highly motivated to produce a better plan. J Allard, a good counter balance to Todd in many respects, played a special role representing the XLT in this portion of the planning process.

ACRONYM STARTER KIT

Members of the XIG had to continue their work on the existing Xbox business, develop their group's plans for Xenon, and participate in the XIG review process for the comprehensive thirty—make that eighty—pager. This was a difficult task encompassing three jobs in one, but engaging key individuals from across the team was absolutely essential. Luckily, we had strong leaders and great teams because that's what it takes to build great products. And the comparison with our original "planning" for Xbox and the outcomes of that process was an ebony-to-ivory contrast.

Beyond producing an innovative yet practical plan, the XIG provided an ancillary benefit by forcing disparate parts of the organization to work more closely together on important elements of the program. Over time, as members of the group reviewed various aspects of the plan, they gained a greater appreciation for the challenges faced by other groups, how components of the plan had to mesh, and the necessary tradeoffs. The XIG became the "us" in a battle with "them," the XLT, in their efforts to gain our approval for their approach. While never a fully cohesive group, the XIG represented a second level of leadership within the Xbox team with a collective stake in the outcome. Given the United Nations nature of our origins, this was extremely important when we entered the execution phase of the project.

Along the Xenon trail, we discovered some tools that enabled the XIG to progress. First among these was a concept J Allard called BXT—Business, eXperience, and Technology (presumably, "BET" didn't sound cool enough or was already taken as a TV network name). In selecting people to own various aspects of the Xenon project, we struggled to find leaders that had the expertise to cover the full breadth of a particular issue. At times, a leader would have excellent sales and marketing skills and understand the ins and outs of the P&L but lack the right sensibilities to work with the development team. In other situations, a strong technical leader would come to the forefront but quickly demonstrate insufficient skills in thinking through the commercial aspects of an issue or managing across teams.

After hitting our heads against this wall for a while, we concluded the XIG needed a balance of those who were strong in the business, user experience, and technical attributes of the project. The sub-groups creating specific plans within the thirty-pager needed the same type of balance. Sometimes the group leader would be the B person, while at other times, it could be an X or T leader. In one important case, Xbox Live, we had three co-leaders representing each part of the BXT equation. "Three in a box" is certainly not a best practice for group leadership, but forcing ourselves to cover all aspects of BXT in every working group was important to the project's ultimate success.

The second tool popularized during XIG planning was the idea of Key Initiatives or KIs. In crafting the thirty-pager, the XIG broke the problem into smaller pieces with KI teams attacking each section. This approach divided the work and allowed many members of the XIG to play leadership roles on important aspects of the project, significantly improving quality and buy-in to the final plan. Each KI's piece was subject to review and stress testing by the rest of the XIG before it was incorporated into the overall plan, while at the same time, other KIs were required to adjust as new elements of the plan became clear.

The KI concept created a very dynamic planning cycle with good peer review and better team dynamics, as everyone recognized that all elements of the plan would get a detailed review. KI's are probably the most elementary tool presented in all of *Xbox Revisited*, but when the team is hunkered down deep amidst the trees, it is very helpful to rely on common-sense concepts that force you up to see the forest.

The final acronym tool involves what Microsoft used to call world-class "individual contributors," or ICs. I've talked at great length about the need for strong leaders to drive complex projects successfully, but in this phase of the work, projects also need specialists who are uniquely qualified to complete critical elements of the plan. These often underappreciated team members possess the specific skills and domain expertise to bring the broader vision to life in a rich and effective way and should be valued appropriately. For example, the music for Halo was scored by a Bungie founder named Marty O'Donnell, who was spectacular at creating just the right mood and backdrop for the various elements of the Halo game. I never thought of that as

> Plans are great, but it's the artists, technicians, and craftsmen who actually build great products.

a critical-path item in a product plan, but it was absolutely essential to Halo. Likewise, in the midst of an online Halo firefight, everyone takes network security for granted, but the contributions of Dinarte Morais, one of the best software security developers in the industry, were significant in the success of Xbox Live. Plans are great, but it's the artists, technicians, and craftsmen who actually build great products.

Not all working groups like the XIG lead to positive outcomes. Many end up being bureaucratic duds, usually because of misaligned goals among group members, poor leadership, or both. I've been responsible for a few of these groups that feel good but get nothing done, and the process is not easy to manage. But if they are structured and led properly, independent committees can work through problems in an interdisciplinary fashion that takes everyone's needs into account, while recognizing that the broader objectives of the task must still be met. Some groups never make it all the way to the finish line, but even then, much of the work they've done can be used by others to identify remaining issues and craft solutions.

Our own XIG process suffered from some of these challenges and was far from smooth. As in many aspects of the Xbox universe, we were making up the rules and processes as we went along. There was always a sense that we were doing the right thing, but never a sense that we were actually doing it correctly. As an example, I never developed an efficient or satisfactory way for the XLT to review the XIG work on a regular basis, which led to considerable frustration and decision-making constipation. This was a further example of J Allard's "go to the river and bring us back another rock" metaphor for ineffective leadership.

I concluded somewhat late in the process that we should have provided the XIG group and its individual leaders with input and feedback while trusting them to make final decisions in many important areas. A great leader should spend the bulk of his or her time establishing strategy, communicating that strategy, and managing the people responsible for driving it to a successful conclusion. Leaders need to trust that strong group managers will use a well-designed framework to make the right decisions most of the time. If a weak link making poor decisions is discovered, that portion of the chain needs to be replaced quickly. Anything else runs the risk of deteriorating into "seagull management"—swoop, poop, fly the coop—and that is not a recipe for success.

THE 300-PAGE FRONTIER

Our deep investment in the XIG planning process began to pay off as we entered the execution phase of the Xenon project. As is often the case, trial by fire and difficult operating challenges tend to burn away the dead wood, leaving a highly skilled team behind. Although the original Xbox experience was filled with challenges, the Xenon team learned many lessons from those issues and built a significantly higher and deeper level of expertise within our operating functions. Not everyone on the team was able to make the transition, but I certainly felt more confident in our skill set than I did at that disastrous first E3 presentation. Over the course of the intervening four years, we went from a team of Triple-A players to major leaguers with a number of all-stars within our ranks.

The Xenon thirty-pager, which morphed into a much longer PowerPoint deck, paved the way to the 300-pager, the final element in the 3/30/300 strategy process. Not surprisingly, the full set of specifications for Xenon was more than 300 pages long, and I'm quite certain there was at least one additional zero in the page count. This last frontier of the 3P Framework required day-to-day execution skills from the leader all the way down through the various levels of management to the entry-level members of the team. These individuals were the final keys to implementing a winning strategy because their jobs encompassed all the details that made up the core elements of the project plan.

Successfully communicating the strategy to each member of the team was an important aspect of rolling out the plan. At the outset, the key components of the 3P Framework and the thirty-pager that went with it had to be well understood and accepted by a broad cross section of the team. There is nothing worse than doing great planning work that is unclear to the day-to-day workers or to individuals who are allowed to take what Washington, DC, calls a "pocket veto" and ignore elements of the plan.

Effective communication takes place via the more formal emails, memos, group meetings, and speeches, but also includes a healthy amount of "in the daily course of business" communication that results from leaders who are visible to the team. People need to hear the message frequently and in person from senior leaders in the organization. It's also important that managers demonstrate their commitment to the plan in all types of environments. The phrase "everything communicates" is totally true.

As the planning progressed, we developed a two-way street of information traffic. The framing of specific elements of the plan exposed inconsistencies and issues the local experts needed to flesh out and reflect in the larger 300-page plan. Being open to changes from below was an important part of this process. The culture also had to reinforce strong interactions among the various sub-teams. Like many groups, the original Xbox teams got caught in a giant game of telephone. Instead of talking directly, messages got passed back up the chain of command so they could be sent down to other teams. That game never ends well.

Beyond great communication, the 300-page team had to turn up the power of the microscope to ensure that every element of each complex system was designed properly. Attention to detail became incredibly important because it's often the smallest items that create the largest issues. That first Xbox had over 1,100 components, and any one of them could cause problems.

In September 2001, a few months before the first original Xbox units were sold, the Xbox team discovered a manufacturing problem with the Xbox DVD drives. The process for securing the drive in the box was modified as production shifted to the main assembly line, and now under certain circumstances, the drive developed a heavy vibration that produced a loud, rattling noise. And, believe me, the original

Xbox had plenty of heat fans already making noise. The engineering team had to scramble to come up with solutions for the boxes already manufactured and invent a longer-term fix that still enabled high-speed production. All of those changes were disruptive, and none of them were cheap.

A maniacal focus on the specifics in a plan is important for another reason: this attention to details produces moments of surprise and pleasure for customers. In part, Apple has been successful due to their ability to get the details right in a way that absolutely captures imaginations. We take it for granted today, but remember the first time you used a touch gesture on a screen and something simple yet amazing happened? That smile on your face made Apple special.

Managing expectations and making tradeoffs was another element of this detailed planning phase. As the team sought to achieve the high goals established in the 3/30 plan, reality raised its ugly head and reminded us that everything was not possible. When planning a product, you have three dials to consider—cost, features, and schedule—and, unfortunately, only two of the dials can be used at any one time. In the case of the original Xbox, we chose to optimize for features and schedule, designing the most powerful console in the market with a fixed ship date of November 2001. With Xenon, we shifted gears and focused on cost and schedule, in large part driven by the principles and priorities we established in the three-pager. This move from features to cost generated a dramatic, positive shift in our P&L, enabling Xenon to reach and ultimately exceed our lofty profit goals.

PERSEVERANCE WON'T QUIT

I've described a simple yet elegant strategic process that brought Xenon from a gleam in a silicon engineer's eyes to the Xbox 360 product ready to launch. The 3P Framework, Rule of 3s and 5s, 3/30/300, BXT, KIs, and ICs are all important concepts that enable teams to create a plan for success, especially when the challenges they face are exceptionally complex or daunting. In a meritocracy, having the best plan and the right ideas should guarantee you some level of achievement. But the world doesn't work that way, and success requires more than just the highest IQ. For the Xbox team, as for many others, that extra element was a simple yet elusive ingredient: perseverance.

Perseverance is more than trying harder—Avis, after all is still #2, which J Allard was fond to remind me, is just the first loser. Perseverance in business is analyzing a challenge, developing a plan, executing on that plan, evaluating the results, and then changing tactics until success is achieved. This level of effort certainly involves plenty of work, but more importantly, it is about investing energy in a smart, directed way that has the opportunity to lead to new, better outcomes. Persistence requires the unique ability to bounce back from setbacks, vault over obstacles, and blow through roadblocks. If the first version of Xbox was about scaling difficult mountains to scramble to the starting line, the transition to Xenon and Xbox 360 was about perseverance, the search for a way past the mountains on to a higher plain.

Anyone who was an early Xbox 360 customer will understand the phrase "the red ring of death." During the first year of Xbox 360 sales, we began to receive customer complaints about Xboxes shutting down and refusing to start back up again. Three of the four ringed lights on the Xbox faceplate would light up red, and the machine would just stop dead in its tracks. Although this general failure error indicator could have signaled a variety of different problems, the volume of issues kept climbing and reached a point where we knew we had a systemic issue. Unfortunately, finding the root cause of the problem was remarkably difficult. Our efforts involved our very best engineers, external consultants and physics experts, some folks from academia, and teams from our chip suppliers. While the product continued to sell well, the customer-service volume continued to rise, and we needed a comprehensive approach to the situation.

Leaders from all of the affected teams met in the basement of my house one evening in May 2007 to finalize a plan for addressing this issue. While I can't remember why we met under those circumstances, this was clearly a crisis situation. Finance, marketing, operations, business management, and development leaders were all there to review our status and make a decision. At the end of a long, difficult conversation, we took a deep breath and decided to extend our warranty to three years and repair or replace every console affected.

While this was clearly the right thing to do for our customers, the implications were profound. Every team in the group would be affected, essentially doubling everyone's work. In addition to developing and testing a fix for the problem, we had to create an entirely new operations system to receive, repair, and return millions of consoles. This was an entirely new business operated by the existing team and funded by a $1 billion write-off approved by the Board of Directors and announced to Wall Street. In the midst of this, we had to make sure that we continued to sell Xbox 360 and gain ground on Sony.

I didn't sleep much that night or for many nights to come. As a leader, you always wonder how you and your team will respond in difficult circumstances, and I was profoundly proud of what the Xbox team did after that decision. First, they accepted responsibility for the problem. We had created a terrible experience for our customers, and it was our job to fix it. The hardware team took the lead here, quietly digging in to create several new generations of consoles that eventually eliminated the problem. The operations team moved mountains to set up the systems to provide a quick, quality experience for customers needing their consoles repaired, dealing with the endless set of specific issues associated with each claim. Our sales and marketing team continued to promote and sell Xbox 360 effectively, actually gaining market share during the period.

Undoubtedly, the red-ring-of-death experience was painful for our customers, but they rewarded our efforts to solve the problem with remarkable loyalty, and our customer satisfaction ratings actually held steady during this period. As for the team, our unwillingness to let this problem knock us down saved Xbox 360 from the jaws of defeat. Personally, I was hugely disappointed and humbled by the entire episode, and that angst left a mark on me that exists today. Nevertheless, the perseverance of the team and their intense efforts to do the right thing for our customers were a source of great pride. And stepping back from the specific emotions of the situation, I learned that even the best-run projects will have these types of issues—and the real test of a leader and a team is their ability to rally to the cause and do the right thing.

> I learned that even the best-run projects will have these types of issues—and the real test of a leader and a team is their ability to rally to the cause and do the right thing.

PLANNING FOR TOMORROW

By their very nature, most strategic frameworks cover multiple years, which enables those doing the detailed plans to consider their work in phases. A good plan not only makes tradeoffs between features and capabilities but also across years. Many of the most important capabilities of Xbox did not ship with the original product, including the Xbox Live environment, and yet very few people remember that first year without multi-player gaming. It is equally easy to forget that the iTunes music store was launched eighteen months after the original iPod, and the App Store was released a year after the first iPhone shipped.

A corollary to this planning principle is that every plan should incorporate a disciplined approach to measurement, evaluation, and recalibration. A high-performing team will get about 85 percent of the product or service right the first time. The secret sauce is having systems in place to understand shortcomings and provide improvements and new capabilities that close the gap toward 100 percent quickly and seamlessly for the customer.

If a company or product that has a first-mover advantage also does a great job adding enhancements, it is difficult for others to enter the market successfully. To go back a long way in history, Lotus produced a spreadsheet called Lotus 1-2-3, which was an industry-defining product on DOS-based PCs. However, when the market moved to graphical user interfaces (Macintosh and Windows), Lotus was slow to improve their initial graphical offerings. In fact, in the time it took them to do one update to their Windows product, the Microsoft Excel team did multiple new versions of a product already superior in features to what Lotus had to offer. While this was not the only reason Excel ultimately dominated in the graphical era, it was a major contributor to Lotus' demise.

Taking a 3P Framework plan and turning it into a living document that evolves with the project, market, and competitive situation requires integrating the strategic process with the operating rhythm of the company or organization. This important stage involves translating the framework into an annual plan, including objectives, budgets, headcount, and measurement metrics. The operating plan can be built from the bottom up or from the top down—and many high-functioning organizations actually do both to drive integration and build in checks and balances in the process. There is a vast library of literature on developing high-quality operating plans and measuring results. In my common-sense world, this boils down to a practical process involving the following steps that should be completed at regular intervals—usually once a year depending on the organization and the circumstances:

1. Develop and Communicate 3P Framework
2. Translate Five Priorities into Annual Operating Plan and Metrics
3. Communicate and Execute Operating Plan
4. Review Performance Relative to Metrics
5. Evaluate Changes in Situation: Internal, Competition, Market, Customers, etc.
6. Review Five Priorities and Adjust Appropriately
7. Develop New Operating Plan and Communicate to Team
8. REPEAT

While the purpose and principles portion of the plan should only change on rare occasions, it is important to revisit these cornerstone concepts periodically, both to validate them as well as reinforce them to the team. Over time, a team that can establish the integration of its strategic rhythm with its operating cycle dramatically increases its likelihood of success in the market.

Once we were in market with Xbox 360, much of the team shifted their full-time attention to this operating cycle. And while the three-pager and the strategic planning progress laid a strong foundation, this operating team added tremendous topspin to a positive situation. While I was still responsible for Xbox during this period, my role expanded to include related areas like music, video, TV, and mobile phones.

New leaders, including Peter Moore, who joined us from Sega, and Don Mattrick, who came from EA, both led the team with distinction during this period and contributed numerous innovations through-out the Xbox 360 life cycle. Among these was the development and introduction of the Kinect sensor, which extended the useful life of Xbox 360 by several years. The team also dramatically improved our operating model and grew both sales and profits. The Xbox 360 was the flagship console product in the market for eight years and is just now winding down. The team released its latest Xbox generation, Xbox One, in November 2013, and the fight with Sony continues in high gear.

The Xbox light may not have turned on way back on May 16, 2001 at our E3 debut, but it shone brightly for ten years of my career at Microsoft. I'm thankful every day for the opportunity I was given and for the incredible people who taught me so much during that exciting time. Moving beyond Microsoft, I have embraced the 3P Framework we developed and incorporated the difficult lessons learned about the planning process into my personal Act II. There is a crying need for common-sense approaches to complex issues—especially to address major challenges in our community and civic institutions. I call this work "civic engineering" and have committed myself to evangelizing solutions to these problems in my post-Microsoft, post-9/11 career. The 3P Framework and 3/30/300 worked in the virtual worlds of vid-eo gaming and, I believe, can help us address the challenging realities we face in the world.

7

RETURNING TO GROUND ZERO

As part of the Xbox journey, I traveled to New York frequently for meetings and conferences, including to complete my original press tour just two weeks after 9/11. While the trips have become less stressful with time, whenever I'm there, I think about waking up to the destruction and sadness that morning in 2001. For me, the connection between Xbox and events across our country is more than just about a physical location at a time in my life. Although I wasn't thinking of it this way at the time, our epic sojourn from New York to Seattle fundamentally changed my attitude toward the importance of civic issues, and more particularly the direction of our country overall.

While sandwiched into that Ford Taurus with three acquaintances that were quickly becoming friends, I wrote a journal chronicling my thoughts and experiences. In hindsight, the journal was another link in a chain that reconnected me with my early dreams of writing a book, giving back to others, and being a civil servant of some sort. These journal excerpts set important context for my focus on a strategic framework for our country:

Events of the past week have certainly saddened, angered, and perhaps challenged all of us. I arrived in New York at 6:00 a.m. on the morning of September 11. There really aren't words to express what happened in New

York and Washington DC. I grieve for those who died and for those who lost loved ones. I marvel at the courage firefighters and police are showing to rescue and help others. I'm amazed at the stories of survival of those who have been pulled from the destruction alive. And I am confident that we will rise a stronger, if perhaps less naïve, nation that will demonstrate its unity, strength, and belief in peace triumphing over hate.

I wanted to write a quick narrative to let everyone know of our experiences in NY (there were several of us there) and share some thoughts on our country. While I never felt threatened, it wasn't easy to go to sleep that Tuesday night—it was very surreal to look out over Times Square at 10:00 p.m. and see almost nobody outside, and then turn back to the TV to see the horror again and again . . .

On Wednesday morning, James Bernard and I made the decision to drive out of NY. James got to the rental car agency at 6:30 a.m. and picked up the car he had reserved immediately after the first plane attack—fortunate for having acted quickly—since there were a dozen other people waiting in line who didn't have reservations and couldn't get cars. He was in contact with April McKee, and ultimately drove down to lower Manhattan to pick her up as well. In the meantime, I got in touch with Craig Suhrbier, a friend from our church, who decided to come with us. So, by 11:30 a.m. on Wednesday, the four of us stuffed our luggage into the trunk of our Ford Taurus and began our cross-country odyssey. We had five cell phones, one pager, four laptops, several books, and a full tank of gas . . .

Rather than go through the full travel log, I'll just say that we took I-80 and I-76 west on our way to Pittsburgh to catch flights we had booked in the hopes that airports would re-open. About halfway there, we decided that we were going on to Chicago instead . . . and eventually, we just kept driving. So we hooked up with Interstate 90 outside of

Cleveland—and from then on we stayed on I-90 all the way to Seattle. We stopped for about five hours at an Embassy Suites in Chicago. We left there at 8:00 a.m. Thursday morning and drove straight through to Seattle, where we arrived around 2:00 p.m. on Friday, for a total travel time of fifty-one hours. Along the way, we had some interesting experiences and observations:

Mobile Homes: Our car started out as a standard equipped Ford Taurus. Of course, this was insufficient for our band of travelers. We quickly realized that we had a serious cell phone problem: nobody had a recharger adapter for the car. So, in Butler, PA we made a trip to a Radio Shack (every town has one) and they, of course, had just the right adaptor that worked for four out of five of our phones. We were now ready: our humble car was prepared to battle the night and the long miles. But on day two, we realized that we had made one mistake. So we stopped at the Rushmore Mall Target (just to prove that we are equal opportunity consumers) to buy four pillows for the long night ride through the Rockies. With that, our car was a fully equipped all-country travel vehicle . . . and it faithfully returned us safe and sound to Seattle.

Gas Stations: Of course, we made lots of stops for gas along the way. Our first stop was at a Stuckey's truck stop (convenient because we missed the entrance to the PA Turnpike). We also saw several Sinclair gas stations—I had forgotten about the purple dinosaur assuming that it was extinct (OK, that was hard to resist). We also saw Conoco, Citgo, Exxon, Amoco, and the other standards (another bad joke for history buffs). Perhaps my favorite was in Oacoma, South Dakota (which for those of you geography majors is just outside of Chamberlain, SD). This was what we call a full service station: gas, food, bathrooms, and . . . a casino in the back.

Xbox: On the way out of that Rushmore Mall we ran into a Software Etc. that had all of the Xbox materials up in the store—including empty console and game boxes and a bunch of merchandising. We stopped in to take a picture, and Derek Barnes, one of the store clerks, came up and asked us what we were doing. We had a great conversation with him about how Xbox was selling. He said that pre-sale and reservations for Xbox were going great and that all the managers in the store had ordered one. He said that DOA3 and Halo were the two leading games thus far, and added that he'd been up looking at Fever and was going to buy it (along with NFL 2K2). So . . . we know that we have a good footing in Rapid City, SD—empires have been built on less. [Author's note: Derek and I stayed in touch for many years, sharing video game stories and family life.]

Radio: Throughout the trip, we listened to the radio, usually looking for news channels to hear what was going on in NY and DC. Along the way, we got to hear a good cross section of "Americana," including some amazing talk show conversations—such as the award-winning "catch 'em, shoot 'em, or catch 'em and shoot 'em" discussion. We also had a brief interlude with South Dakota Public Radio Jazz Nightly—or "Jazz Music for Cattle." Perhaps the most touching was our ability to listen to the entire prayer service held at the National Cathedral . . . an amazing, moving moment even across the airwaves with just the words and music.

The Land: Probably the most impressive aspect of the trip was just seeing the country. I was really surprised at how pretty Pennsylvania is. I grew up in Wisconsin and was reminded how beautiful that state is. The Great Plains, although not exciting, are very impressive in their own way. All of this reminded me of the amazing geographic diversity of the US and how fortunate we are to live here.

Perhaps in all of this narrative, you've lost track of why I wrote this epistle. I've lived all over the US. I grew up in the Midwest, went to high school and college in North Carolina, and lived in Florida, Washington DC, New York, and California before coming to Seattle. But this was the first time I've driven across the country and really seen America. And I realized that somehow during the last thirteen years in Seattle, I've lost track of some very basic truths about our country.

America is a place of amazing diversity—diversity in people, land, customs, faiths, ethnic backgrounds, and many other areas. Events in New York and Washington, DC, along with our sojourn across the country, reminded me how important that diversity is. It showed me how we can use that diversity as our strength . . . as a way to unite together in a clear cause for justice and peace. And it reminded me that our diversity and liberty are not "free." They are treasures we have to earn and fight for each and every day. So as you go through the coming days, take nothing for granted, cherish those you love and what you have been given, share it freely with others, think about those that have gone before you, and be prepared to defend and fight for your freedom.

God Bless America . . .

Each year on 9/11, I reread my journal and share an email with my three compatriots who put up with me all the way home to Seattle. We are bound at the hip by our joint experience, and I think often about what I learned from them and our travels during our shared pilgrimage. I inevitably shed a tear or two. Ground Zero, our cross country trip, and my 9/11 journal have become the metaphor for my transition from business leader to citizen activist, from Chief Xbox Officer to Civic Engineer.

A CIVIC REPORT CARD

My new work as a civic engineer begins like most new efforts should: with an evaluation of the current state of affairs across our country. Evaluating some objective and comparative measures provides important data on the general state of the nation, and a few examples are also instructive. There are some challenges to overcome in this evaluation, as there is less uniformity than there was in the singular Xbox story. In the civics world, the quality of work done at the local and state level varies widely, economic circumstances look very different if you are in California compared to Michigan, and cultural norms and expectations diverge in multiple directions. Part of the beauty of the 3P Framework is that it can be applied successfully across all of this diversity.

Measuring civic engagement is a good way to understand how seriously citizens take the responsibilities and opportunities provided in our democratic system. At the most basic level, voting is a core civic duty. Expressing our will through the elective process is an enduring way for voices to be heard. On the one hand, there is an expanded use of citizens' initiatives and propositions, in particular in the western states, that has increased community involvement and decision making in the governing process. Whether this produces good laws is an interesting debate, but it definitely indicates a willingness and desire for involvement on the part of some citizens.

On the other hand, over the last fifty years, voting rates in federal elections have averaged only 50 to 55 percent in presidential election years and 35 to 40 percent in nonpresidential years. Sadly, this low voter turnout places the US well behind other countries, which average above 70 percent participation. While there are differences in political systems that account for some of this variance, the fact remains that many Americans are not exercising one of their core rights and obligations as citizens.

Voter apathy turns into distrust and disagreement when it comes to our government institutions. US congressional approval ratings (as measured by Gallup) have never been strong over the past forty years, vacillating between 20 to 40 percent over that period with some peaks in the low 50-percent range around the turn of the century. Given that most representatives receive only about 50 percent of the vote in an election, this is not terribly surprising. Over the last few years, however, the trend has shifted downward dramatically with the congressional approval rating hitting an all-time low of 9 percent in November 2013. It's difficult to imagine how an organization with single-digit approval ratings can be viewed as the legitimate representative of the people's will—harder still to imagine its members as leaders of the country. Certainly, rates for specific leaders, including the president, would vary from this collective abyss, but the fact remains that Americans have lost respect for their elected governing bodies.

To understand and evaluate the financial underpinnings of our civic institutions, Mary Meeker's report "USA Inc.: A Basic Summary of America's Financial Statements" is an excellent resource. Though the report is now several years out of date, the basic trends and issues have not changed. The problem begins with an electoral system dominated by special interest groups, spending levels designed to influence election results, and pressures on all candidates to say "yes" to as many people as possible. That paradigm leads to an attitude that the government can and should try to solve most problems, creating more programs and spending more money. Unfortunately, there is little emphasis on determining what works and what does not, programs are rarely discontinued, and leaders are unwilling to say "no."

The net result is a government footprint in our economy that has expanded dramatically from an average of 3 percent of GDP prior to 1930 to a peak of 25 percent in 2010, and a current level of 22.5 percent. To fund this footprint, we have taken on a debt that has doubled over the past thirty years to 53 percent of GDP. If you include a host of unfunded liabilities, that number grows to 94 percent of GDP and is projected to approach 150 percent of GDP over the next twenty years. Any company or nonprofit organization operating on this economic model would be out of business very quickly.

In a number of other important policy areas, progress has ground to a halt. The front pages of our newspapers are dominated by important international events, crimes, and natural disasters. The attention-grabbing nature of the urgent is natural and understandable and an important source of information for citizens. However, the urgent crowds out the important and reduces our ability to deal with fundamental issues. What we really have is a systemic head-in-the-sand and kick-it-down-the-road approach to problem solving that can best be described as "Reform Interruptist." Why deal with a real problem today when you can allow someone else to deal with it tomorrow? The tax system, healthcare policy, immigration laws, gun regulations, election rules, and infrastructure investments are all areas in need of dramatic reform that have been postponed seemingly indefinitely.

On a more positive note, Americans demonstrate their community engagement in ways outside of what would be considered traditional civic and government activity. They are more involved

> What we really have is a systemic head-in-the-sand and kick-it-down-the-road approach to problem solving that can best be described as "Reform Interruptist."

in nonprofit activities and give more money per capita than in any developed country in the world—and no other country is even close. According to the National Philanthropic Trust, 88 percent of US households give to charity, and the inflation-adjusted total amount donated to charities has more than doubled over the last forty years. Volunteerism is likewise strong with over sixty million Americans providing over fifteen billion hours of service.

This propensity to engage in community needs and activities is a towering strength in our culture and an asset that can be leveraged even more effectively to address some of our more challenging issues. Beyond the engagement of businesses and governments, nonprofits and their volunteers represent a powerful, well-respected force, creating a third pillar to support action and progress. I've seen the amazing impact this engagement drives through my work with the Boys and Girls Clubs, both locally and nationally.

Perhaps a good way to summarize this report card is to look at two case studies in local communities I know well to understand the dynamics at play.

THE MICROBREW SOLUTION

I was raised on the north side of Milwaukee, WI, in a comfortable, suburban community with good schools, close-knit families, and traditional values. In my mind's eye, it was an idyllic time filled with sports activities, nights of Capture the Flag, and plenty of bike riding in the neighborhood. I won a sectional championship in Little League, explored the shores of Lake Michigan, and experienced my first kiss. Once the brewing capital of America, Milwaukee has gone through wholesale changes over the succeeding thirty years, many of them positive and some more challenging.

By 2006, Milwaukee had the dubious distinction of having the nation's second highest teen birth rate amongst the fifty largest cities in the country, second only to Philadelphia. A group of concerned community organizations, led by the United Way of Greater Milwaukee, banded together in 2008 to form the Teen Pregnancy Prevention Initiative. They set a goal to reduce the teen birth rate by almost 50 percent by 2015. To achieve this aggressive target, they developed an integrated strategy that focused heavily on working with partners across the civic and social landscapes to influence teens. The United Way worked with the Milwaukee Public Schools, the University of Wisconsin, the city of Milwaukee's Public Health Department, and a broad base of public health affiliated nonprofits in the city.

They raised funds from local charitable foundations, corporations, and local media companies to fund a large, aggressive public awareness campaign. This campaign included advertising, YouTube videos and quizzes, and an integrated website that delivered blunt messages about teenage sex and teen pregnancy. Milwaukee Public Schools changed its human growth and development curriculum to incorporate stronger messages related to sex and reproduction, and all groups worked aggressively to encourage teens and parents to discuss sexual issues early and often.

The results have been dramatic, with teen birth rates dropping by over 50 percent in five years, eclipsing what was thought to be a stretch goal two years ahead of schedule. By focusing on partnerships, the lines between nonprofit, government, and corporations blurred, and the organizations united around an approach that had remarkable success. The partnership element of this strategy is particularly important because different organizations were able to bring a variety of skill sets to the table. This is an excellent example of what many call "collective impact" and demonstrates the results that bold, strategic civic activity can deliver.

A BRIDGE TOO FAR

Unfortunately, the progressive work in Milwaukee is just one example in a sea of missed opportunities. The city of Seattle, WA and surrounding King County have a difficult commuting problem to solve. Through lack of historic foresight, the region's transportation system is heavily focused on car traffic supplemented by a bus system. There is a small amount of regional rail activity and a new light rail system that covers a de minimis percentage of the geographic area, but the area's mass transit system pales in comparison to systems in New York, Chicago, Boston, or even San Francisco. To make commuting matters worse, building roads in the area is complex and expensive because of the Puget Sound, several large lakes, and numerous hills.

Access from the east side of the county to Seattle is concentrated on two floating bridges across Lake Washington, one of which, the 520 floating bridge, is well past its useful life and well over its designed capacity. This is a regional disaster of earthquake magnitude waiting to happen. For almost twenty years, the city, county, and state have been engaged in an effort to develop a solution for this problem. The short answer is that some elements of a new bridge are under construction. The longer answer is a testament to a lack of comprehensive strategic thinking on the civic challenges we face.

The 520 Bridge was built in 1963 and transformed the east side of Lake Washington from a farming and summer vacation area to a thriving city and residential area that is now the home of almost 300,000 people. All of this growth has put tremendous pressure on the 520 corridor, both from a capacity perspective as well as in terms of the lifespan of the bridge. As early as 1990, it was clear that capacity needed to be expanded and the bridge replaced. With multiple levels of government involved, concerned community groups organized, lobbyists and anti-tax groups engaged, and the pressures associated with elections, no plan was approved for the bridge until 2011, when tolling began to fund a new bridge.

In the interim, multiple studies and proposals were considered and rejected, traffic conditions worsened, and the cost of replacement went up. Today, construction is almost complete on the east side of the approaches and significant progress has been made on the new floating bridge deck. However, there is still no agreement on how to fund, construct, and connect the new six lanes to Interstate 5 at the end of the bridge corridor. This is the traffic-planning equivalent of pouring water into a funnel and hoping it won't overflow. In 2015 or 2016, King County will be the proud owner of a new six-lane bridge that moves traffic more effectively from the east side only to block it equally effectively with the old four-lane corridor on the other side of the lake. It is an interesting experiment in how to spend billions of tax payer dollars with no clear destination in mind. This lack of strategic management and foresight is symptomatic of the broad range of civic issues that are either being mismanaged or not addressed at all.

> Conflicting priorities, special interest politics, fragmented responsibilities, inconsistent and misleading communications, and poor leadership all conspire to disempower the very people the process is designed to serve."

What is fascinating and frustrating about this example is that the average citizen, the typical voter in this community, understands completely how ridiculous the situation has become and yet seems resigned to the futility of their circumstances. Conflicting priorities, special interest politics, fragmented responsibilities, inconsistent and misleading communications, and poor leadership all conspire to disempower the very people the process is designed to serve.

The challenge before us is how to change this perception, unlock citizens' natural understanding of common-sense compromise, and engage them in creating better outcomes. When obvious problems fail to attract rational solutions, we need to dig deeper to understand the source of the problem. Much like our discussion of the dysfunctional Xbox team, many of these issues return to a fundamental root cause: the failure to establish a clear project vision (purpose), rules upon which tradeoffs and decisions can be made (principles), and specific actions that must be completed to achieve success (priorities). The 3P Framework developed during the Xbox journey and inspired by that 9/11 trip across the country can be an essential part of improving our civic processes and building better local, state, and national outcomes.

8

THE FIRST P:
A CONSTITUTIONAL PURPOSE

I've always loved history and civics—in middle school, I devoured books about historical events, and I can remember debating issues with my mom all the way back in the eighth grade. I grew up listening to Tom Brokaw in the morning, a journalist who has subsequently dedicated much of his career to reporting on historic and civic issues within a unique, American context. My high school dream of being a United States Senator was deeply rooted in my character and upbringing.

That upbringing taught me that a representative democracy requires that individuals stand up and be counted to drive productive, constructive change. That means debate, dialog, and engagement, not only among elected officials, civic employees, and nonprofit board members, but everyone. With the end of my Xbox experience, I began to envision a path to influencing change in the world beyond Microsoft. As I pondered the next phase of my life, I could see that the strategies we developed for managing the Xbox business had the potential for much broader applications. The 3P Framework offers a common-sense approach to addressing complex problems—on any level—even in the rarefied halls of the US Congress and the Oval Office. Purpose, principles, and priorities form an ideal scaffolding for business plans, civic initiatives, and even the formation of a country.

WE THE PEOPLE

If writing a purpose statement for Xenon was difficult, I struggle to put myself in the shoes of the founding fathers as they contemplated the fledgling nation's many challenges while it was governed loosely under the Articles of Confederation. Just eleven years following the signing of the Declaration of Independence and only a few years removed from a bloody, consuming war with the British, the nation was deeply fragmented, struggling economically, and facing an uncertain future.

Fortunately for today's Americans, despite many divisions and differences of opinion, they worked together to lay the foundation of our country over two hundred years ago, a groundwork that has definitely survived the test of time. In creating the US Constitution, they recognized the need for clarity of purpose, most likely because the Articles of Confederation were viewed by many as nothing more than a treaty between the thirteen states. Taken with a more modern interpretation of the words, the preamble to the Constitution provides a strong statement of purpose worth a more detailed 3P Framework analysis:

> We the People of the United States, in Order to form a more perfect Union, establish Justice, insure domestic Tranquility, provide for the common defence, promote the general Welfare, and secure the Blessings of Liberty to ourselves and our Posterity, do ordain and establish this Constitution for the United States of America.

We the People: Although I'm not a constitutional scholar, this phrase is perhaps one of the most quoted from the US Constitution and reinforces the very fact that this is a democracy. The US is a country led and governed by people we entrust with certain powers. Those we elect bear a tremendous burden to provide faithful and effective leadership. Of course, those who vote for these elected officials need to be responsible and thoughtful in their decision making. In many ways, our government succeeds or fails on this very concept.

Perfect Union: The goal of a perfect union requires balance, with each group playing its appropriate role. In today's context, state and federal authorities must understand their established roles and fulfill those roles faithfully. Even though tension is inevitable and at times useful, leaders need to stay in a "constructive zone" where collaborating on solutions is the norm. At present, the dialog is moving in the wrong direction with confrontation and gridlock being more the practice.

Establish Justice: Justice is about the equal, fair, and open treatment of individuals. It is also about the appropriate judgment and punishment of those who violate the rights of others or laws of the land. Despite a strong Bill of Rights and related amendments, our track record on justice is actually quite mixed. Historically, we have trampled on the rights of Native Americans, African Americans, women, and many other minorities. At the same time, our commitment to relative transparency, free press, and public trials/appeals has demonstrated that justice is ultimately possible. The Thirteenth, Fourteenth, Fifteenth, and Nineteenth Amendments, The Civil Rights Act, and Title IX are all examples (if belated) of meaningful social change driven by a justice-led agenda.

Insure Domestic Tranquility: This is closely related to the establishment of justice but focuses more specifically on creating a stable, safe environment. Given the context of a country that had just survived a brutal war of independence, this was clearly an important phrase for the constitutional framers. In our era, domestic tranquility certainly can be applied to public safety, infrastructure, and economic/class issues.

Provide for the Common Defence: On the surface, this clause clearly refers to a national militia (or a coordinated set of state militias) that provides for the defense of all states in the union. In a more modern context, this concept includes managing and protecting our borders and conducting relationships with other countries. We frequently broaden the defense mandate to include military bases and armed engagements around the world, with notably mixed results. As the wars in Iraq and Afghanistan (to say nothing of Vietnam) demonstrate, we need to think very carefully about the definition of "common defence."

Promote the General Welfare: In many ways, this is the most vexing and difficult phrase to evaluate because of its breadth and openness to interpretation. It certainly encompasses things like providing for an efficient infrastructure within the country and ensuring that basic services are provided in an appropriate manner, and it also promotes helping those who are most in need. At the same time, the founding fathers did not want to "ensure" the general welfare or relieve individuals of their personal responsibility for their own welfare. Perhaps that is literary nitpicking, but the fact remains that every word is important when writing a purpose statement.

Secure Liberty: Freedom and choice are important elements in our American culture. From these concepts come our emphasis on individual rights and many of the freedoms embodied in the Bill of Rights. The government's job is to protect these liberties and respect the rights of individuals. As recent NSA and CIA controversies high-light, the path between the Common Defence and Securing Liberty is a difficult course to navigate.

To Ourselves and Our Posterity: This somewhat antiquated phrase is easily overlooked, but it is a critical part of the constitutional purpose. Clearly, the founders recognized that government is responsible both as stewards for current citizens as well as for the long-term welfare of the country. In our rush to avoid today's problems, we too often ignore the difficult decisions and investments required to ensure the strength of our country for future generations. In fact, we have gotten into a very consistent and bad habit of kicking problems down the road for other generations to manage.

The Xenon and US Constitution purpose statements are obvious-ly tackling different types of issues and certainly problems of different scale and import. As much as I love Xbox, shaping the future of our country was and is a tad more important. Despite these differences, they both provide something that is essential to solving difficult, complex problems and managing change. Each statement defines the important pillars of a foundation and in the process sets the context and the parameters around which the rest of a strategy can be built.

In the case of Xbox, frankly, our goal was very basic—moving from the fringes of the market into the mainstream where we could compete on a more level playing field with Sony and Nintendo. In the case of the Constitution, the goal was much more lofty and signifi-cant: creating a living and evolving document that defines a country and reflects the needs of its people, welcomes new citizens to the fold, and invests for the future well-being of all.

AN OLYMPIC EXAMPLE

Defining purpose is almost more important to nonprofit and civic organizations than to businesses because they generally don't have other focusing mechanisms like income statements, stock prices, or shareholders. The United States Olympic Committee presents an interesting example of this concept. Founded in 1894 and federally authorized by the US Amateur Sports Act of 1978, the USOC is responsible for the training, entering, and funding of US teams for the Olympic, Paralympic, Youth Olympic, Pan American, and Parapan American Games. It also serves as the steward of the Olympic movement throughout the country. Since it receives no federal funding, the USOC must raise from private sources, over $800 million over each four-year period that encompasses a summer and winter games cycle.

With 120 years of history, the USOC has seen its share of organizational ups and downs. Even within the past thirty years, there have been at least three commissions established to evaluate the USOC's performance, address organizational issues, and propose changes to its structure. In March 2010, the most recent of these commissions, led by former NFL Commissioner Paul Tagliabue, proposed some fine-tuning to the organizational structure, including increasing the size of the Board of Directors and balancing its composition to ensure all constituents were represented. The report also recommended that the USOC's new CEO, Scott Blackmun, perform a review of the organization's mission statement and propose appropriate changes. I joined the USOC Board of Directors just after the Tagliabue report was issued and was very impressed by the leadership demonstrated by both Scott and the Board's chairman, Larry Probst, in response to that report.

Scott Blackmun was hired by the board in the disappointment and aftermath of Chicago's failed bid to host the 2016 Summer Olympics.

With the USOC roundly criticized for its role in this failure, Scott had many issues to address, some of which were urgent, some of which were important, and some of which were both. To his credit, while making a broad range of required changes, Scott took the time to step back from the situation and worked with his board to evaluate the USOCs strategy from top to bottom, including its mission statement. Getting the board, the USOC staff, and its sports constituents clear on the organization's mission—its purpose in the 3P Framework—was an essential step in changing the USOC's strategic course.

The USOC's mission statement in 2010 was "To support U.S. Olympic and Paralympic athletes in achieving sustained competitive excellence and preserve the Olympic Ideals, and thereby inspire all Americans." While on the surface this seemed reasonably clear, it left unanswered some important questions about the focus of the USOC and the criteria it should use to evaluate resource allocations. One of the primary tasks of the USOC sports performance team is determining how much money, time, and training resources to allocate to various sports and athletes. With forty-seven National Governing Bodies (NGBs) for Olympic sports, another twenty-six NGBs for Paralympic sports, and thousands of athletes in the Olympic performance program, this funding exercise is incredibly important and appropriately closely evaluated by USOC board members, NGBs, and athletes. The 2010 mission statement could be read to prioritize sports and athletes with Olympic medal potential, but it could also be argued that the way the phrase "Olympic Ideals" was used indicated that all sports should receive meaningful resources.

The USOC board discussed and debated changes to the mission statement, both in committee settings and in several full meetings. Scott also sought input from leaders across the NGB and athlete community in addition to representatives from those groups who were already on the USOC board. After much discussion and evaluation of draft proposals, the board focused on the "inspiring all Americans" portion of the mission statement. While we all love a good, tear-inducing Olympic story, Americans, being Americans, are inspired by winners. With that in mind, the new (and current) USOC mission statement makes it clear that the organization is focused on sustained competitive excellence: "To support U.S. Olympic and Paralympic athletes in achieving sustained competitive excellence while demonstrating the values of the Olympic Movement, thereby inspiring all Americans."

What is most instructive about this example is how small the changes were to the mission statement and yet how large an impact those changes had on the organization. The new mission statement made it crystal clear that the USOC would focus on competitive excellence, shifting the emphasis on Olympic values toward the concept of competing and winning in the proper way.

Certainly, not everyone was happy with the new mission, as this was the foundation for increased transparency and changes in resource allocations. Some sports and athletes received less funding since their podium potential was deemed lower for a variety of reasons, while others received the same or increased resources. This was certainly jarring across the movement and led to a number of difficult conversations. However, there was no longer any confusion, obfuscation, or ambiguity, and that has been a tremendous benefit to the overall US Olympic family. This transparency also has

> This was certainly jarring across the movement and led to a number of difficult conversations. However, there was no longer any confusion, obfuscation, or ambiguity, and that has been a tremendous benefit to the overall US Olympic family.

enabled the USOC staff to make decisions in a quicker, more accurate, and more timely fashion because they have a clear knowledge of the foundation for those decisions.

Look at any charitable organization in this country, and you will find a mission statement, in part because a statement of charitable purpose is required if you want to file as a nonprofit with the IRS. Yet governmental entities such as city councils, state legislatures, and various agencies often operate without this essential first P of a strategic framework. And even nonprofits don't always consider their mission as an essential part of their strategy. It didn't take us long to discover at Xbox that if you don't define your purpose, you don't know what you're doing or why. And the result usually ends up like Seattle's half-baked construction plans for the 520 Bridge.

XBOX LESSON NUMBER ONE

Hammer out a purpose statement before you begin any strategy construction.

9

THE SECOND P:
IN SEARCH OF A PRINCIPLED GOVERNMENT

As much as our work on Xbox reinforced my view that principles are an essential element in any strategy, the concept of "principled politics" never registered in my consciousness, and I certainly never considered writing a set of principles for our national leaders. That changed as I was reading Doris Kearns Goodwin's *Team of Rivals*, chronicling the origins of Abraham Lincoln's cabinet and the decisions he made to navigate the Union through the Civil War.

Lincoln was an impressive leader on many fronts, but I was most struck by his discipline and willingness to evaluate decisions based on a set of concepts that defined how he should lead the country. Even though his presidency was marked by careful navigation through mine-filled waters and ultimately many compromises, Lincoln always stayed true to the core ideas he felt were important. In 3P Framework terms, his purpose was to hold the Union together, return the Confederate States to the Union, and prevent the expansion of slavery beyond its original boundaries.

After years of debate, public speaking, and extensive writings on the issues of the time, Lincoln had developed a set of core decision-making principles that enabled him to test various courses of action. As an example, he certainly believed that keeping the Border States in the Union was an essential element to saving the country over the long term. And he was willing to make allowances in certain policies and decisions that flowed directly from that viewpoint, even if they angered or frustrated ardent supporters of abolitionist objectives. What appeared to be indecision or delaying tactics by some critics were actually proactive acts to live within the principles he'd established while pursuing his ultimate purpose.

If we fast forward to today's policy debates, much of the problem is that we don't actually discuss or debate the principles themselves. Instead, we declare them as a "truth" that can be used as a crutch, and in some cases as a weapon, to justify our decisions or chastise those made by others. The discord created by the wars in Iraq and Afghanistan demonstrate this issue clearly. What are we willing to do in the name of fighting terrorism? How do we feel about the inevitability of civilian casualties as a result of military action? What requirements do we have of local leaders in exchange for their support? How do we define success?

In the absence of clear answers to these questions, we struggle to have coherent, productive discussions about the advisability of various actions, and achieving consensus on policy direction becomes next to impossible. In a world dominated by Internet news, hashtags, and social media feeds, we've lost the willingness to step away from the keyboard and actually question the core ideas underlying various issues and points of view. We've lost the art of the constructive debate that seeks agreement on some central ideas that we can use to evaluate decisions. We are a nation in search of our principles.

TIMELESS IDEALS

With two hundred years of rich historical precedent and plenty of evolutionary revolution in this area, proposing a definitive list of American principles is definitely hazardous duty. I certainly claim no particular expertise in the area other than I'm a thoughtful citizen who cares deeply about his country. And perhaps that is the point. Americans need to have a set of ideals in mind as they evaluate the quality of their leaders and the effectiveness of the strategies they purport to pursue. We can't have a meaningful discussion on any policy issue until we've fully explored the role of government and the principles upon which it should operate. Without some form of consensus on these principles, leaders can't even decide which issues are most important, much less how to address them. Until the conversation is elevated to this level, we will continue to struggle with a fragmented body politic and government gridlock.

Just as I drafted the principles for our Xenon efforts, I will accelerate the civic debate by proposing five operating principles for our government. They flow from the purpose outlined in the preamble to the US Constitution and are consistent with our history, culture, and common sense:

1. ***Creating Opportunity:*** The government must play a strong role in making the United States the "land of opportunity," and that prospect must be available to everyone. Part of creating this environment is building, maintaining, and upgrading the physical and intellectual infrastructure required in a modern society. Beyond that, our civil rights history has largely, and correctly, been focused on creating opportunity for disadvantaged or discriminated groups. Opening the right to vote to all citizens, the long, belated Civil Rights Movement in the 1960s and Title IX are good examples of pursuing equal opportunity, and even in these areas there is much more to be done. Although I'm not sure the original framers of the Constitution had this in mind, providing a safety net that

supports those most in need is an essential element to leading a modern society. This approach generates an ongoing tension between creating opportunity and trying to ensure equality of outcomes. The government cannot afford to manage, ensure, or orchestrate outcomes effectively, nor should it try. Actual outcomes are a function of individual skill/effort, social and market forces, and the laws of chance and providence. Establishing the boundary between opportunity and outcomes is a difficult balancing act, but one that must be achieved.

2. *Living within Our Means:* The government should never run just like a business, but responsible government requires a recognition that revenue and expenses are related and financial results must remain within certain boundaries. The government has to live within its means with revenues and expenses growing or shrinking in a synchronous way. Of course, the government can and should borrow to finance some spending activities. In particular, in times of crisis, debt provides real, economic leverage and is actually valuable for the country. But just as with personal or business affairs, this borrowing must fit within certain limits. At the state and local levels, real constraints exist, both constitutionally and practically, that force and maintain this equilibrium. For the federal budget, however, few structured safeguards exist, so it's imperative to establish and follow a self-imposed, rational business model that supports today's needs but also preserves economic strength for future generations.

3. *Investing for the Future:* If the goal is to "insure domestic Tranquility" and provide for "our Posterity," the planning-time horizon must

shift significantly. For far too long, the US economy has expanded based on an underlying premise of cheap credit, high consumption, and government policies that have supported and accelerated this approach. Even though this leads to periods of episodic growth, it also sets the stage for the inevitable collapse, the latest of which deeply wounded and divided the country. Going forward, investment, innovation, and production must be engines of growth rather than counting on short-term fixes that amount to nothing more than Band Aids. Leaders and voters need to have the patience and foresight to invest in programs and policies for the long term and give them enough time to germinate and grow.

4. *Balancing Rights and Responsibilities:* To a remarkable level, the founding fathers focused on establishing the rights of individuals and delineating between the rights and responsibilities of the states and the federal government. In addition to the core of the Constitution, the Bill of Rights and several other amendments make clear that the social contract with all levels of government is based on the premise that citizens come first. The government certainly must pass laws that regulate behavior, build underlying infrastructure, and arbitrate between groups and individuals. But these roles should be reserved for as few things as necessary to "promote the general Welfare." The corollary to this principle is that there should be as little government as is required to fulfill our purpose and that as many issues as possible should be left to individual states or private citizens to arbitrate as befits their local circumstances. Unfortunately, we have allowed federal and state governments to infringe on this principle too frequently.

5. ***Fostering the Melting Pot:*** The United States has an incredible history of welcoming and integrating new citizens, new cultures, and new philosophies into the "American Way." Wave after wave of immigrants, beginning with the Jamestown colony and the Pilgrims right through to the current Hispanic, Asian, and Eastern European migrations, have come to our country looking for a new start. African Americans arrived against their will and have faced tremendous discrimination, but they have persevered nonetheless. Although these cultural combinations often involve real tension and acrimony, we somehow manage to find our way to a broader consensus. Each new group enriches our culture, our intellectual capability, and our human resource in different ways, and that is a tremendous source of strength. While not easy, continuing to welcome newcomers in spite of real security issues and imagined insecurities is important to long-term growth and prosperity.

By their very nature, articulating a set of core ideas invites discussion, debate, and disagreement. Given the size and diversity of the country, full consensus is probably not possible or even desirable. As an example, there will certainly be those who argue for a stronger role for the federal government, and that is a discussion that has been going on since before the Constitutional Convention in 1787. If it hasn't been resolved in 225 years, we are probably not going to wrestle it to the ground today. However, the debate itself is incredibly useful and helps us understand other points of view and consider compromises and alternatives without the hard constraints and complications of specific laws or legislation. It also forces the thought process above the trees to consider the entire forest, an activity that is all too often lost in the rush of an Internet-driven world requiring immediate answers.

In the 3P Framework, it is absolutely essential that teams and organizations engage deeply in this phase of discussion because without it, they run the almost certainty of irreconcilable differences arising during the priority-setting phase. This lack of agreement definitely handicapped our early Xbox efforts and made all elements of our work more difficult. If there is no agreement on principles or at least some understanding where there is mis-alignment, the rest of the strategy setting process will be badly compromised.

ETHICAL DILEMMAS

I learned how to write properly in the tenth grade. As part of an advanced language arts and social studies curriculum, I wrote a fifteen-page, typed thesis paper as a semester-long project that would form a major portion of my grade. Since I was an explorer of history and my father had served in the Pacific Theater during World War II, I decided to write a paper justifying the use of the atomic bomb at Hiroshima and Nagasaki.

This type of ethical dilemma forms a great backdrop to understand principles in a civic context. Imagine for a moment that you are Harry Truman, a relative unknown who rose to the presidency by default when President Franklin Roosevelt died in April 1945, just as the war in Europe was ending. But the fight with Japan in the Pacific continued, and while his electoral mandate was unclear, Truman's purpose was certainly to end that conflict quickly. As it became apparent that the Manhattan Project had produced a weapon of unimaginable power, the question for Truman was whether to use it.

Making this type of difficult decision where many forces are operating in different directions requires a clear declaration of principles. While my thesis paper justifying the dropping of the atomic bomb is long lost, I can recreate the principles Truman must have pondered as he considered his options to fulfill his purpose of ending the war in the Pacific:

1. ***Saving American Lives:*** Americans, including my father, were already training for Operation Downfall, the land invasion of Japan scheduled for October 1945. Estimates for Allied casualties in that invasion ranged from one hundred thousand to one million, and given the way Japan had fought at Iwo Jima and Okinawa, nobody doubted this would be a long, gruesome fight. And casualties would have been significantly higher for the Japanese, who were training civilians to participate in the defense of Japan.

2. ***Changing the Japanese Political Dynamic:*** While Japan was technically ruled by an emperor, the military was clearly in control and determined to fight to defend the homeland. There was also the cultural element of "saving face" that needed to be considered, given Allied demands for an unconditional surrender. That mindset needed to change in a dramatic way to make an early surrender possible.

3. ***Exacting Revenge:*** Although perhaps not a popular principle to articulate, Truman was well aware of Americans' feelings about the sneak attack at Pearl Harbor that killed thousands and the anguish experienced by those who'd lost siblings, children, and parents during the fight across the Pacific. He also knew how US POWs

were being treated, or mistreated as the record would demonstrate, and one could imagine his desire to exact some retribution.

4. *Ending the Economic Drain in the US:* Although not well understood or publicized, financing the war was a significant challenge for the US government and continuing that burden with an extended campaign in Japan would create even greater difficulties. Moving on economically required a reduction in military spending.

5. *Limiting the Soviet Advance:* The structure of the post-war period was already taking shape in Europe, and it was clear that the Soviet Union was no longer going to be an ally. With Soviet forces poised to invade Korea and move down the peninsula toward Japan, Truman must have considered the implications of having them involved in the post-war reconstruction in Japan. The longer the war in the Pacific continued, the more likely this would become a reality.

The destruction of Hiroshima and Nagasaki were horrible events, ones that brought the world into the nuclear era unprepared for what would follow. "Planning for the nuclear age" and "protecting the lives of Japanese civilians" are noticeably absent from my hypothetical Truman principles. In the former case, it's unclear anyone had the foresight or self-awareness to factor nuclear proliferation into the decision; in the latter situation, Americans had already deeply internalized all Japanese as the enemy. For Truman, this was a no-win situation that traded one set of horrors for another.

We recently found a letter my father wrote to his parents the night after he visited what remained of Hiroshima in October 1945.

It perfectly captures the devastation and sadness in Hiroshima, but it also reflects the relief he felt that the horror of the war was over:

The street car crossed a bridge, rounded a corner, and there it was—nothing but complete and utter destruction as far as you could see; except for a few modern buildings or what was left of them, it was as flat as a pancake. Even those still standing had nothing left but four walls; no doors [or] windows, and a blank inside for the most part . . . All this devastation was done by one atomic bomb a single man could carry . . .

As simple as all that, the area was totally devastated; it'll take generations to rebuild Hiroshima if they ever try and then it'll be one hell of a job. All I can say is that if this is any indication, the human race will destroy itself; it's hard to believe even after having seen it.

Hope & pray we get good orders—stateside orders; it won't last forever anyway.

My father saw the horrors of the war in the first person from Iwo Jima to atomic destruction, but he never spoke to us about his experiences in Hiroshima. My mom found the letter after he died. The nightmare of war changes people in ways others can never fully appreciate. I wish I'd understood that better at the time.

> The nightmare of war changes people in ways others can never fully appreciate. I wish I'd understood that better at the time.

I am quite certain Truman never thought about this situation in a 3P Framework context, but these types of complex dilemmas can only really be evaluated based on the principles the 3P Framework demands. In my thesis paper, I focused heavily on evaluating Truman's decision in the context of the information he had and the circumstances he faced in social, economic, and geo-political terms. I also discussed the moral dilemma created by the explicit need to trade off some lives for others. Historians have explored and questioned everything from Truman's motives to his grasp of the implications of the decision, and many have concluded he erred. I, on the other hand, concluded that using the atomic bomb was a justifiable act and am thankful my father and other young men never participated in Operation Downfall. Either way, working with sound principles does not ensure perfect decisions—only disciplined ones.

A TWENTY-FIRST CENTURY DILEMMA

Evaluating principles based on historical armchair quarterbacking is one thing. As we experienced during our Xbox journey, developing principles in real time takes enormous foresight, leadership, and self-awareness. An analysis of a modern dilemma that is ethically challenging in its own way will expose these issues more clearly.

US immigration policy has been troubled for a number of years across a wide range of issues. Most recently, however, there has been a wave of undocumented immigrants, including over 50,000 children, who have flooded our border area, creating a large refugee community there. They are fleeing gang violence, poverty, and abuse in Honduras, Guatemala, and El Salvador and seeking protection and asylum in the US. President Obama and Congress have traded proposals, barbs, and condemnations, but ultimately they haven't agreed on any constructive action to address either the humanitarian crisis or the more fundamental immigration issues we face. The president has proposed taking unilateral executive action, which has been met with disdain and dismay from both parties.

Immigration is more than just about citizenship; it is actually an economic growth, foreign policy, humanitarian, national security, and citizenship issue. Because the policy choices available are complex and cut across the needs of many constituent groups, it is not surprising that attempts to jump to the answer have failed. Instead of "leaning in," leaders need to step back from the fray and discuss the core principles on which broad immigration policy must be based. With this as context, specific options can be debated and common-sense middle ground discovered. I would suggest the following principles to form the basis for that discussion:

1. ***Driving Comprehensive Reform:*** The time has long passed for Band Aid solutions. Our immigration policy is seriously flawed and needs to be re-worked from top to bottom. This means solving the shortage of H1 employment visas, dealing with permanent residents who are undocumented, and providing a better security framework for our borders. These are related issues that must be addressed together.

2. ***Dealing with the Source:*** Too often our approach to an immigration issue is to treat the symptoms only. In the case of these child refugees, we need to move "upstream" on the problem and address the source of the problems in Central America and work with Mexico to stop the migration before it starts. Immigration is not just a citizenship issue—it is a foreign policy issue as well.

3. ***Capitalizing on the Opportunity:*** Immigrants have contributed dramatically to the strength and growth of our country for over 400 years. A well-designed policy will attract candidates for citizenship

that can enrich and enhance our country with a broad range of skills. Immigration policy is not about exclusion—it must be about fostering the American melting pot. It must also acknowledge and accept that a large number of undocumented residents have lived in the US for many years, already contributing productively to our social and economic fabric.

4. ***Recognizing That Security Does Matter:*** The opportunity also has risks, and protecting the country is part of our government's core purpose. We need to utilize all of our innovative and creative skills to design a policy that protects us from those that wish to do harm. This is not about walls and fences that are easily breached. This is about thoughtful measures that evaluate and qualify citizens in an appropriate way.

5. ***Providing Humanitarian Aid:*** What is often lost in the current discussion about illegal immigrant children is that they are refugees first. They are fleeing corrupt regimes and violent gangs in search of safety. This situation is not unique to the United States, and we must fulfill our obligation to provide humanitarian support and protection. This approach requires a real, sustained allocation of resources and extends the concept of a safety net to those that are forced to our border.

> This is not a debate about opening or closing our borders; rather it is a discussion about the relative value of new residents, the appropriate qualifications for US citizenship, and our capacity for humanitarian action.

A sound immigration policy can be developed based on these principles, or some similar set that is fully debated by those who understand the problem well. That policy will allow more people to become US residents and ultimately citizens—and yet it will also have to exclude those who do not qualify for a variety of reasons. This is not a debate about opening or closing our borders; rather it is a discussion about the relative value of new residents, the appropriate qualifications for US citizenship, and our capacity for humanitarian action.

Much of the dysfunction in our civic institutions revolves around principles that are either opaque or intentionally hidden. Everyone brings their own personal agenda to an issue, and when others don't understand the agenda itself, reaching consensus on actions is difficult to impossible. We saw this clearly during Xbox's formation with the original team carrying a United Nations-worth collection of ideas and concepts that were often unexplained and usually contradictory. Once we had transparent discussions about our principles and agreed on things like "making a profit," "gaming first," and "expanding our audience," developing common-sense solutions to our problems became dramatically easier.

XBOX LESSON NUMBER TWO

Debate, develop, and declare your principles as early in the process as possible—this sets the stage for effective priority setting—the third P in the 3P Framework.

10

THE THIRD P: PRIORITIES, FOCUS, AND THE LINT TRAP

As much as purpose and principles are essential elements in a strategy, the final pillar in the 3P Framework provides the actual direction that tells teams what must be done. Priorities set the agenda and form the transition point from strategy to the annual operating plan. Focused properly, priorities provide great clarity and empower leaders at all levels to make decisions efficiently and effectively.

Equally important, priorities inform and drive the organization to decide what *not* to do over the coming years. They give leaders and their employees the tools to determine when something is off strategy or of lower importance and push it to the back burner or all the way off of the stove. Many of the groups with which I work have projects that are either experiments or considered small, incremental investments that they defend as being "easy for the team to do" or "items we get for free." All of these projects are organizational lint that clog up the system, occupy management time, and distract employees with the urgent rather than the important. There is definitely a reason your clothes dryer has a lint trap. A leader's job is to use priorities as a way to filter out the unnecessary lint in the organization.

STATE OF THE UNION

Perhaps the grandest stage for discussing priorities is a State of the Union address. Section II of the US Constitution requires the president to "from time to time give to the Congress Information of the State of the Union, and recommend to their Consideration such Measures as he shall judge necessary and expedient." Originally, this requirement was fulfilled through a written report, but the advent of mass media transformed this into a joint session of Congress, complete with plenty of pomp, ceremony, and applause. The opposition now even uses this as an opportunity to present its own views on the state of the nation.

In a modern context, this speech is the president's best chance to articulate his strategic platform, both to Congress and to the American people, and to establish key priorities for the coming year. Just as the Xbox team established its business priorities in the Xenon three-pager, analyzing this presidential tool provides insight and understanding to the ins and outs of establishing national civic initiatives. To do this, I reviewed two of President Barack Obama's addresses—his first in February 2009, which was technically just an address to a Joint Session of Congress, and his January 2012 State of the Union speech. What I found was a measure in contrast with interesting implications for the priorities section of the 3P Framework.

The 2009 speech was given in the context of a nation in crisis, complete with a failing banking system, high unemployment, challenging wars in Iraq and Afghanistan, and a lack of confidence across the country. Importantly, the Democrats controlled the White House and both houses of Congress, and President Obama had been elected by a mandate-sized majority, winning almost 53 percent of the popular vote and more than twice the number of electoral votes.

The speech began by outlining measures being taken to stabilize the economy and start the process of recovery—a necessary element given the state of affairs. The remainder of the address presented a remarkably clear explanation of the president's priorities. These included energy policy, health care reform, improvements in education, debt reduction, and foreign affairs initiatives. While it included a few jabs at the previous administration and some pandering to certain groups, it passed the Rule of 5s quite well and demonstrated a real, longer-term vision for what needed to be accomplished.

The 2012 speech could not have been more different. After reviewing some of the administration's accomplishments, it covered a laundry list of initiatives, including jobs in manufacturing, trade policy, job training efforts, education improvements, immigration reform, innovation R&D, energy programs, infrastructure investments, market regulations, tax reform, federal government effectiveness, and defense strategy. It was much more caustic about the tensions between Democrats and Republicans, more explicit about the gulf between Congress and the president, and generally more political than visionary in nature. While that may have served the president's needs at the time, from a strategic framework perspective, short-term myopia and lack of focus are cardinal sins. Not only did it fail the Rule of 5s test, it was a big emotional letdown from the focused and rousing nature of the 2009 address.

These speeches are incredibly important, so missing the mark is very expensive. From experience, keeping thousands of Xbox employees informed on the key strategic directions of the organization was incredibly difficult. I am an effective speaker, and I missed the mark with some regularity. Imagine when your audience is 115 million diverse households with over 300 million people that have as many differences as they do similarities. No matter how elegant, well researched, or "correct" the strategic framework, if the priorities are poorly formed or miscommunicated, the strategy will likely fail. Because of the public nature of the work, this is almost certainly more significant in a civic or political context.

My point is not to critique the president or pick sides in any political debate. I could just as easily have selected two of President Bush's State of the Union addresses and demonstrated the same basic points. The real message is that great strategy requires intense focus on the initiatives that match to the rest of the strategic framework. If you allow other considerations to influence the communication, get sidetracked by specific constituents, or pander to the immediate needs of the day, the entire approach is dramatically weakened. In addition, setting priorities requires leaders to have the courage and perspective to rise above the fray and be dispassionate about what must be done. All of this is especially true in civic and political arenas where the authority structure is less clear than in a business like Xbox. Great civic leaders and strategists find ways to surmount these challenges consistently and raise their audience's awareness of common-sense solutions to a new level.

> If you allow other considerations to influence the communication, get sidetracked by specific constituents, or pander to the immediate needs of the day, the entire approach is dramatically weakened.

MR. FOCUS COMES TO WASHINGTON

As a general rule, I find that the quality of a restaurant is inversely proportional to the number of items on the menu. Producing quality food requires discipline and a real love for the particular items you are serving. Of course, the difficult tradeoff for the chef is knowing when there are sufficient items to satisfy a meaningful cross section of the community while limiting the selection enough to ensure quality. With no disrespect, there is a reason we put Olive Garden and Le Cirque in different categories.

"Focus" is an easy word to say but not something that comes naturally to many business leaders, much less most politicians. Setting priorities, whether you're the president of the US, the Chief Xbox Officer, or the president of your school's PTA, is all about driving discipline and making conscious choices between alternatives. This clarity was a huge challenge for the XLT and for me as the CXO in particular. We certainly had some epic debates and some raucous battles about various tradeoffs that needed to be made. The Xbox project had both tremendous depth and great breadth, creating temptations to want to do it all. But that was a grain of sand compared to the Sahara-sized span of control faced at the federal government level. And there is a sharp contrast between the 3P Framework mantra to "leave some things undone" and standard operating procedures in Washington, DC.

As demonstrated in the 2012 State of the Union Address, "government priorities" is very close to the dictionary definition of an oxymoron. If businesses struggle to establish a crisp list of five core initiatives, it's unclear to me if the term "priority" is even understood broadly in political circles. Governments generally, and our current leaders

> Governments generally, and our current leaders in particular, do not value the importance of tradeoffs and the value of saying "no."

in particular, do not value the importance of tradeoffs and the value of saying "no." If the United States is to have any hope of addressing the core issues across our country, leaders must develop the willpower and capability to determine what is critical and important, and which things they are not going to pursue.

To demonstrate that civic focus is possible, even at the national scale, I propose five priorities that comprise the essential elements of a 3P Framework plan for a promising American future. My guess is that most readers will agree with some, question others, and wish that still others were replaced with some contrary proposal. While I believe passionately in these specific ideas, the more important point is to have a real debate about priorities, decide what is important, and pursue those policies and ideas aggressively:

ECONOMIC COMMON SENSE

At the core of the debate over priorities lies the fundamental dysfunction in the country's business model. Many of the nation's challenges begin and end with questions about economic status; poor education, crime, obesity, addictions, government dependence, and family dysfunction all are positively correlated with poverty. The simple act of getting and holding a job that pays a living wage has a tremendous impact on individuals' lives and on the economy collectively, and employment is the most powerful tool to reduce the wealth gap that is driving a schism in our social framework. Consequently, improving our employment environment is an essential element in restructuring our economy.

In fiscal terms, while spending levels have continued to grow, both in absolute terms and relative to the size of the economy, there has been a corresponding set of pressures to limit tax increases; provide tax incentives for various programs; and support certain special interest groups, industries, and classes of individuals. As any economist, business leader, or head of household will tell you, continually increasing expenses and constraining revenue is a recipe for disaster. The US economy can certainly support more debt than most, so this is not a proposal for a balanced budget. Instead, it is focused on bringing balance to the budget. On current course and speed, according to one likely scenario from the Congressional Budget Office, entitlement expenses and interest on the national debt will consume 100 percent of government revenues by 2025. Even if this is off by five years one way or the other, this is a serious problem.

The solution involves, at the same time, complexity and common sense and definitely requires some courage. We must be willing to rethink defense, Medicare/Medicaid, Social Security, and other entitlement programs that account for roughly 75 percent of today's federal budget. At the same time, we must recognize that tax revenue (and tax rates for some) must increase. In short, the government must develop a more balanced, sensible economic model for operations. The National Commission on Fiscal Responsibility and Reform (otherwise known as the Simpson-Bowles Commission) summarizes it this way: "After all the talk about debt and deficits, it is long past time for America's leaders to put up or shut up. The era of debt denial is over, and there can be no turning back."

EDUCATION TRANSFORMATION

A Chinese proverb wisely says, "When planning for a year, plant corn. When planning for a decade, plant trees. When planning for life, train and educate people." If the goal is to change the course of the country's development, America must lead the world in educating young people. And yet we have gone from a nation with one of the best overall education systems to one that struggles with the basics of reading, writing, mathematics, and science. We are now ranked twenty-seventh in math scores and twenty-second in science, according to OECD data. Twenty-five percent of high school age students will not graduate, and the social and economic costs and implications of that failure are staggering. We are raising a lost generation of children. As Frederick Douglas said, "It is easier to build strong children than to repair broken men."

Urgent reform is required to reinvent our approach to education, and that reform has to start by measuring and rewarding quality teaching and removing those who are not good at their craft. Taken as a whole, students don't spend enough time on the core academic subjects that matter and lose ground over an overly long summer break. Students must be reached at the critical pivot points in their education, in particular in early learning and in sixth to eighth grades. Finally, post-secondary training is often a better path for many young adults than an expensive, four-year institution. Reshaping the education system is a long-term infrastructure project that will require patience and consistency to show progress. It also will require collaborative work between school administrations, teachers/unions, community service organizations, and parents. Enough money is already allocated if it is spent wisely and focused on the areas that matter most.

ENVIRONMENT AND ENERGY INVESTMENT

This discussion begins at first principles: mankind is having a meaningful and largely negative impact on the Earth's environment with carbon emissions and the subsequent warming of the planet as the most serious issue. It is time to get over the inconvenient truth and work to solve the problem. At the same time, America's lack of a sustainable, independent energy supply is a constant drain on the country and a source of many security concerns. In combination, climate deterioration and unsustainable energy policies will over time make it difficult to provide proper food and water and will negatively affect economic growth with particular impact on the poor.

Ultimately, this is where the environment and energy create a perfect storm of need: developing energy sources that are environmentally sound, domestically sourced, renewable, and economically practical must be a key objective to generate sustainable growth and broader economic prosperity. This effort requires a dramatic increase in core science and technology investments with the government tripling or quadrupling the amount of money it awards for core research—research that should be conducted in partnerships involving the public sector, universities, and private enterprises. Since this approach will take time to yield practical fruits, conservation will be an important and required part of the strategy, along with the utilization of transitional technologies like natural gas to generate interim energy solutions. In the process, the usage of coal as an important energy source must be eliminated due to its environmental side effects. When it comes to the environment and energy, everyone must ask this question: "Twenty-five years from now, will our surviving children look back and say, 'What were they thinking?'"

EQUAL OPPORTUNITY SUPPORT

None of these challenges is as complicated or emotional as the need to provide for those who require assistance. There absolutely is a moral imperative to understand the needs of those who are less fortunate and develop ways to help them. Chronic unemployment, homelessness, and hunger describe some of the most basic challenges to address, but there are others, such as mental health, addictions, abuse, and parentless children. These problems must be attacked in a manner that is fiscally responsible and leads to an improved circumstance for those receiving aid, so that over time, they can become self-sufficient.

Programs must change from "entitlements" (and the social attitudes that go with that word) to enrichment programs that enable people to scale up. While the government certainly must play a significant role in this process, current state and federal programs are plagued by inefficiencies, duplicative design, and generally poor outcome measurement. Healthy partnerships are required among government, the private sector, and nonprofits to build a durable and scalable safety net that truly provides equal opportunities to as many citizens as possible.

To create this system, every program must have a set of criteria and metrics that are measured and tracked to make sure money is being spent effectively. This outcomes-based approach will enable the removal of programs that are not performing and offer enhancements to those that produce results. In the end, providing everyone with an opportunity for success boils down to a human choice. Again, we must ask ourselves the basic question: "If I were in their shoes, how would I want to be treated?"

GLOBAL ENGAGEMENT

Whether we like it or not, the world is a scary place, and one of the federal government's primary roles is defense. While I am not a fan of engaging in needless conflicts, we have to invest both militarily and diplomatically in protecting our interests—and those interests absolutely involve activities in other countries. The ongoing conflicts in the Middle East, the latest twist in our relationship with Russia, the crazy leadership in countries like North Korea, and the risks associated with terrorism and nuclear proliferation are all real threats to the American people.

Protecting our citizens successfully requires an effective military capability, world-class intelligence gathering, and constructive diplomatic skills. The goal is not to be the world's policeman, leading arms dealer, or global bully—the time for those attitudes has long passed. Instead, we should focus our energies on identifying threats to American security, building appropriate partnerships that advance our regional interests, and supporting humanitarian efforts when appropriate.

International affairs is about much more than just providing protection—in fact, it includes promoting global trade, opening new markets, and supporting third-world development, all of which are essential to economic growth. In many respects, our economic strength and business success is both dependent on foreign policy success and one of our best and most important foreign policy tools. Developing and supporting prosperity, both at home and abroad, is a powerful way to win friends and create influence beyond our borders. And in deference to our economic common-sense priority, all of this can be accomplished for significantly less money than we are spending in this area today.

These priorities are a logical progression and reflection of the purpose and principles articulated in the 3P Framework for America. Just as the 3Ps from the Xenon strategy formed the foundation for the creation of

> It should be clear that this is neither an exclusively Democratic or Republican agenda. Instead, it takes a broader view of what is in the best interests of the country and paints a picture that is independent of most orthodoxy and doctrine.

Xbox 360, these 3Ps can form the foundation for an American revival (see Appendix B for the compiled American three-pager). It should be clear that this is neither an exclusively Democratic or Republican agenda. Instead, it takes a broader view of what is in the best interests of the country and paints a picture that is independent of most orthodoxy and doctrine. In the hands of strong, committed leaders, such a common-sense plan could drive lasting, transformational change.

AN ALTER EGO SPEAKS

Ask yourself this question: Do you know any major elected officials or candidates who are willing to tell you with an appropriate level of precision their top five priorities? And if you think they can, ask yourself a second question: Will they say the same thing when they are talking to the next group? Finally, will they openly articulate specific issues that are less important and not on their radar screens? Watching Mitt Romney's campaign for president was like watching a very old game show, *What's My Line?* As the host used to say, "Will the real Mitt Romney please stand up?"

Whether you are running a family business, local government, or building the next generation of Xbox, taking a clear point of view on important issues is an absolute requirement. The fact that others will disagree with you is only natural and something that is an integral part of the testing process for any strategy. Rather than resisting these debates, great leaders embrace them as an opportunity to ensure that the best combination of ideas is incorporated into a final strategic plan.

Naturally, each principle deserves debate and refinement, and each priority demands a detailed plan. In many ways, this is precisely the point of a democratic system. Existing leaders and candidates for public office identify the things they believe are most important for the community, and voters get to decide whether they agree. The problem we face is that we've lost the ability to articulate what is important and then discuss the issues clearly. If the 3P Framework forces that debate, it will have achieved its purpose.

To drive the point home, and to avoid monopolizing the podium, I want to share an additional letter I received from Charles Roscovitch, presenting some alternative priorities. It's useful to consider his viewpoints and imagine the constructive debate we will have at our next get-together:

September 23, 2013

Dear Robbie:

Many thanks for allowing me to read your draft manifesto on America's strategy for the future. It's clear that you are passionate about both the framework and your ideas for addressing the challenges we face in our country. As you know, I certainly share your concerns about our current direction and agree that now is the time for real leaders to stand up and make a difference.

With all of those niceties aside, you and I would attack these problems in very different ways. Let's begin our discussion with the economy, because we both agree that this is at the center of many of our challenges. While your point about a rational balance in our revenue and expenses sounds nice, it just isn't practical in the current situation. When the economy is struggling, you can't cut spending and increase taxes and expect a good outcome. You will end up feeling better about your "discipline" but with an economy that is stagnant or worse.

The government must play a central role in providing stimulus spending to support economic growth and jump start our business engine. I agree with you that we should focus these expenditures on productive infrastructure and programs that prepare others for new forms of work. Thankfully, many economists, including Paul Krugman, argue that our economy is big enough to support expanded deficits for the foreseeable future, and our position as the world's reserve currency insulates us from some risks associated with higher debt levels.

Your emphasis and call to action for leaders is commendable, but the reality is that elected officials effectively run our country. And since we both agree that the officials being elected are largely ineffective, incompetent, or worse, fixing the election process must be a high priority. When special interests from outside an area can legally influence (and at the extreme, buy) an election, we need to rethink how we approach the entire process. I dare say that if the founding fathers realized that billions of dollars would be spent each year to elect certain individuals to office, they would collectively roll over in their graves.

Take the situation of someone elected to a two-year term in Congress. Basically, their re-election campaign begins the minute they're sworn into office, and everything they do is subject to the question, "What does this mean for my chances of staying in office?" With this Damocles hanging over their heads, how can you expect any Congressman or Congresswoman to lead effectively? Of course, the additional problem is that smart, dedicated community and business leaders understand this as well and conclude that running for office is a fool's errand. The net result is weak, ineffective leadership that cares more about their jobs than doing what is right for the country. There is no easy fix for this problem since many of the precepts are embedded in the US Constitution, but we can't ignore the problem and hope it will fix itself.

I agree with your basic message about a strong safety net, but I worry that your approach is a bit naïve. The idea that government, nonprofits, and private businesses should work together to create and manage a safety net sounds wonderful on paper—so does full employment, an end to hunger, and peace in the Middle East. As much as you don't want to hear it, the government is going to have to play a leadership role here and most programs are going to be funded and managed by government agencies.

I'm sympathetic to your point of view about government inefficiencies and lack of measurement, but instead of privatizing these activities, we should build better governance into the programs themselves. The nonprofit world is far too fragmented to be an effective force at scale because everyone has their special, personal charity. And I don't trust the vast majority of business leaders who have demonstrated time and time again that their only focus is on corporate profits.

I found your discussion on education interesting, and this is probably the area where our interests are most aligned. Quality teaching is certainly the most important issue, but I also worry that over-reliance on test scores as a teaching quality metric is not a good strategic approach. I also know that lengthening the school day (and school year) has many side effects that will ripple through local communities in unintended ways. I agree this is a long-term investment that will not show fruits for a number of years so we will need to identify some "quick wins" that can demonstrate to people that we are on the right track.

Perhaps what was most interesting was what you left off of your list of initiatives. In a time where leaders are evaluated on their political correctness, it is a brave soul who is willing to say that civil rights, abortion, gun control, immigration, and health care reform are not a priority. Since you and I have discussed these issues in the past, I know you have strongly-held, principled points of view on all of them and believe that there is much to be done in each area. Leaving them off of your list just reinforces the importance of making difficult choices about where we should focus our resources. Your discipline sets an example that far too few leaders are willing to follow.

In the end, you and I disagree on some of the specific remedies as well as the stack rank priority in which we have to attack problems. I suspect that if we sat down and worked this through face-to-face, we could reach a consolidated point of view that would satisfy each of us enough to support it. Perhaps we can get together once you're past the worst of the book editing process and hash some of this out in a more interactive way.

I am glad you responded to my last letter with such commitment and hope that your manuscript brings other voices to the table. Without involvement from a wide range of leaders, progress will be slow at best.

Let's keep the conversation going . . . .

Respectfully,
Charles

While Charles and I will continue to disagree on elements of an American strategic plan, I relish the opportunity to debate all of these points with him in front of an engaged audience that cares deeply about the outcome. This is the long-lost art of public discourse that educates and informs the electorate and enables new options to emerge and choices to be made. Unfortunately, the "conversations" that most people hear today are sound bites from political speeches and the thirty-second negative political advertising that dominates our airwaves. Rather than educating the public so they can take an informed position, these messages are focused on advancing partisan points of view and raising money for candidates of specific persuasions. Ironically, even the political parties themselves can't reach a logical, consistent consensus, and the Republican Party in particular appears to be breaking apart at the seams.

Whether in the role of employee, board member, or voter, our essential task is to find and support the best leaders who can exercise their judgment and decision-making skills to put the correct strategic framework in place.

XBOX LESSON NUMBER THREE

Setting priorities is about debating and reconciling issues, making difficult choices, and achieving common-sense consensus on a crisp plan of action.

THE DANGEROUS LEAP

The 3P Framework is not some sort of defined destination that says the organization has arrived once it is completed. Understanding and defining the challenges, establishing a strategic framework, and debating the difficult tradeoffs and decisions that must be made are certainly critical parts of the process. But many organizations do an excellent job defining the strategic framework, only to fall on their collective faces either in articulating the specific plan or executing on the details. In fact, moving to the implementation phase presents a new set of dangers and requires a different range of skills. This leap to execution is equally dangerous for the smallest business, local civic groups, and all the way up the organizational ladder to our federal government.

Bringing a strategic plan to day-to-day life is yet another opportunity to apply common- sense techniques to difficult problems.

> Going from three pages to thirty pages to 300 pages is about going through the strategic fire into the executional frying pan. The heat on the stove is often more extreme than during the planning process.

Nailing down purpose, principles, and priorities creates the core architecture for the business or organization, leaving unfinished the very real and challenging work of defining the specifics and executing the plan. Team leaders must complete the process by producing the equivalent of the Xenon thirty- and 300-pagers. Going from three pages to thirty pages to 300 pages is about going through the strategic fire into the executional frying pan. The heat on the stove is often more extreme than during the planning process. And this is where, with due credit to Paul Harvey, "the rest of the story" begins.

THE THIRTY-PAGE STARTER KIT

The next step in an American 3P Framework involves writing a thirty-pager to provide more detailed information about the tasks required to implement each priority. As was the case with Xbox, in reality this plan would certainly expand beyond thirty pages, in particular given the scope of the national priorities. The next level of the implementation process, the 300-pager, would develop into specific pieces of legislation, executive orders, and department-level budgets, and, again, this would be a much longer document for the federal government.

Nailing down the particulars in a thirty-pager and implementing the designated tactics is a markedly different process and requires a different skill set than the original strategy development. A good leader constructs his team in such a way that a few "generals" are talented at the strategic aspects of the plan, while other leaders and the rest of the team are highly skilled in specific execution disciplines. As we experienced during the original Xbox work, an unbalanced organization that lacks one side or the other of this equation will struggle to make progress. Sometimes, in particular as companies grow, people need to be replaced or new skill sets added to enable both of these activities to work in harmony.

In Washington, DC, the challenge we immediately face is deciding who is going to construct the thirty-page plan. I know how difficult that was to achieve for the Xbox team within the relative shelter of the

Microsoft umbrella and with generally clear lines of authority and accountability. Given my experience with leaders in the nation's capital, it's difficult to imagine a group of federal government officials getting together and writing any useful document to complement the five national priorities in a 3P Framework. The normal legislative process suffers from many shortcomings and barriers to productive work and is filled with people whose priorities are aligned with personal and political gain. Congress doesn't even have the leadership, willpower, or inclination to approve an annual budget and only sometimes manages to approve a Continuing Resolution, their poor substitute for a budget. Expecting them to do something difficult and strategic would be worse than naïve.

The executive branch certainly suffers from some of the same issues but has the theoretical benefit of a singular leader who can direct a group in a coordinated way. The president could pull key members of his team away from their day-to-day operations to articulate a plan, either through a cabinet-driven task force or through the appointment of ad hoc committees. As with the XIG that drafted the Xenon thirty-page plan, bringing in people with specific expertise in each area would be immensely valuable, especially if they were independent from the executive branch's normal functions.

To act as the yeast in the thirty-page starter kit, a working group would need a concrete charter to evaluate specific areas and make recommendations that the president could articulate more broadly and introduce into the legislative process. This approach has the benefit of taking issues out of the political arena as much as is possible and off the desk of elected (and beholden) government leaders, putting them into the hands of people with relevant expertise from across the thought spectrum. It also enables a wide variety of very capable leaders from business, academia, and the nonprofit sector to participate in an active and valuable way without running for office.

In theory, a commission should be able to do three things that most elected officials cannot do:

1. ***Focus on the long term:*** Given the realities of our election process, government leaders are rarely free to consider generational solutions that won't lead to results until after they've left office. Our problems are deep and structural, requiring commitment and perseverance in approach over many years.

2. ***Make choices:*** None of these issues can be solved without adversely affecting some portion of the public, and certainly many will perceive themselves as being disadvantaged no matter the facts. Solving these problems requires compromise, sacrifice, and choices that focus on the general welfare across the country.

3. ***Frame solutions productively:*** Part of the legislative challenge we face is that most government discussions begin with the political calculus before analyzing the merits of the issue and possible solutions. Commissions can and must turn that on its head to enable productive debate.

Of course, commissions need to have very specific charters with a constrained budget and timeline to complete their tasks. And selecting the leadership is essential to keeping the group on task, while ensuring that many points of view are considered. Finally, it is vital that there is real, concrete commitment to pursue and implement recommendations that come from a commission, including a requirement that legislators vote on those recommendations. Without this, the effort feels good but the outcome leaves a bad taste in our mouths.

THANK YOU FOR YOUR SERVICE

All of these elements can be seen very clearly in the National Commission on Fiscal Responsibility and Reform. Originally proposed in November 2009 by Senator Kent Conrad, a Democrat from North Dakota, the commission was designed to be authorized by Congress to have binding authority in reducing the annual deficit to 3 percent of GDP and addressing longer-term imbalances between revenue and expenses. When it failed to get the sixty votes needed in the Senate for this level of authority, President Obama created it as an advisory commission in February 2010. The commission was chaired by Alan Simpson, a former Republican Senator from Wyoming, and Erskine Bowles, a Democrat and former chief of staff for Bill Clinton. It included eighteen bipartisan representatives from the Senate, the House, and experts in the field.

In effect, the Simpson-Bowles Commission report issued in December 2010 and supported by eleven of the eighteen members was an excellent example of a thirty-pager addressing the Economic Common Sense priority in the American 3P Framework. Even those who voted against it indicated they were in favor of broad portions of the plan but refused to support it due to certain provisions. Clearly, none of the commission's members loved all parts of the report, but it was a logical, reasonable compromise that would move the nation forward on a dramatically sounder fiscal basis. While I disagree with elements of the approach, I would vote for this plan today, and it is required reading for anyone serious about addressing our ongoing fiscal challenges.

Unfortunately, creating an advisory commission or task force equivalent to the Xbox XIG is not some magical fairy dust that ensures success. Apparently, nobody in government cared about the Simpson-Bowles Commission because nothing happened with the report. Leaders said, "Thank you for your service," but the proposals presented some inconvenient truths that nobody wanted to acknowledge. Why was this report—and others like it—not fully debated in Congress? Why did the president not push this as part of his leadership agenda? Why did smart, dedicated people spend their valuable time working on this, and why do they remain engaged on this issue years later? Commissions work only when leaders are serious about the outcome, and despite statements to the contrary, including personal meetings with Simpson and Bowles, neither congressional leaders nor President Obama were willing to lead decisively on this issue.

Although this failure is frustrating and difficult to reconcile, we shouldn't throw the proverbial baby out with the bath water. Commissions and working groups can create the opportunity for an issue to get fully researched, discussed, and evaluated in a way that leads to new approaches. In an ideal world, the independent and bipartisan nature of a commission would allow it to frame the options in a productive way and put more pressure on legislators to deal with the issues at face value. It would also enable better-informed public discourse on these topics. With more effective presidential leadership, the Simpson-Bowles Commission could have led to real, positive change. Perhaps that is why Alan Simpson and Erskine Bowles continue their fight for fiscal responsibility today.

GET THE HELL OUT OF DODGE

I have been to Washington, DC, on many occasions to lobby on Capitol Hill for various business and social interests. I've met with congressional members, senators, legislative aides and staffers, lobbyists, consultants, and policy wonks. Unfortunately, I've had more than my share of bad experiences, generally not because people disagreed with me, but because they were down-right disagreeable. Perhaps the biggest problem in Washington is that many people's priorities are ultimately parochial and self-centered, with most conversations resolving to a calculus about "what's in it for me?"

> Perhaps the biggest problem in Washington is that many people's priorities are ultimately parochial and self-centered, with most conversations resolving to a calculus about "what's in it for me?"

When I leave from one of these trips, I am happy to stomp the dirt off my feet, "get the hell out of Dodge," and take a shower to remove any residual contaminants.

Leaving Dodge and shifting the policy focus to state and local communities across the country affords countless opportunities to create the equivalent of many thirty-page documents to address specific community issues. While I think progress at the local and state governmental levels is still uneven, there is definitely a hierarchy of high-performing cities, counties, and states that have figured out an operating model that works effectively.

Some of our best and most capable leaders are governors and mayors of large cities. Whether you agree with everything they've done or not—and the record is certainly mixed—mayors such as Michael Bloomberg, Rahm Emanuel, Eric Garcetti, and Cory Booker, along with governors such as Chris Christie, Steve Beshear, John Hickenlooper, and Jerry Brown, have provided real leadership in their cities and states, as well as on the national stage. Their actions are sometimes controversial and contentious, but each has been well backed by their constituents, and they have made real progress on the issues they've pursued. While they may not think about it this way, their actions demonstrate the presence of well-conceived thirty-page plans.

Consider for a moment the dramatic changes that have taken place in New York City since the mid-1990s. Under the leadership of Rudy Giuliani and Michael Bloomberg, New York has dramatically advanced its image and improved the quality of life for its residents. Crime has been reduced, civic services have been upgraded, and the city's reputation has been enhanced. During Giuliani's first term as mayor, the New York City Police Department implemented several new strategies, including adopting James Wilson's "Broken Windows" system. This approach emphasized addressing minor offenses such as turnstile jumping, subway graffiti, and panhandling, believing that it sent a strong "law and order" message to citizens. The city also introduced CompStat, a computer-driven system that mapped crime geographically, as well as charted police performance. While Giuliani was mayor, crime decreased by over 50 percent, with murder rates declining by over 60 percent.

Some believe that the previous major, David Dinkins, and the police commissioner, Bill Bratton, deserve much of the credit for this crime reduction. Still others bristle at the style and tactics employed by both Giuliani and Bloomberg, accusing them of being dictatorial and using their own wealth to support their agenda. But the fact remains that progress was made at the local level, even in a political environment as complex as New York City.

The most important point is not to promote any of these local and regional leaders in particular, but rather to point out that it is often easier to make progress away from the Washington, DC, bubble. While mayors and governors are still affected by the electoral and political calculus, they are significantly closer to the problems and voters can monitor and evaluate them more easily. As the political unit gets smaller, the ability to reach consensus and take action increases. And in some of the US priority areas like education, many of the required changes must be driven from the local level in any event so there is a real opportunity to make progress without running the DC gauntlet. Even on topics like environment/energy and equal opportunity, local and regional alliances can explore new solutions with more flexibility to experiment than can be generated at the national level.

TAKE THE PLUNGE

When the DC dance fails us and the local options are not as strong as those in Dodge City or New York City, we have to revert back to more primal approaches—namely getting directly involved through policy activism. This personal dive into the shark-filled waters involves understanding the key topics of the day, developing a point of view on those topics, and communicating and lobbying that viewpoint effectively. In effect, an individual takes authorship over the thirty-page process. A number of Microsoft executives, including Suzan DelBene, who is my congresswoman, have done this by running for public office.

While I have no plans to run for office, I explored this form of policy activism by drafting more detailed proposals for the five priorities in the American three-pager. This is the civic equivalent of J Allard writing the first draft of the Xenon thirty-page document. And like J's first effort, this personal engagement may prove inadequate in the specifics, but it should serve as a starting point for serious discussions. Hopefully, a more detailed discussion of the education priority will demonstrate the bare minimum necessary to create a thirty-page policy roadmap.

EDUCATION TRANSFORMATION

The decay in our education system is one of the saddest tales of the past twenty-five years, and reshaping this system is an essential element of any plan to improve the core premise of our American dream. Unfortunately, we are failing to educate or prepare our children for productive adult lives. Roughly 25 percent of students are NOT on track to graduate high school, and the number is close to 50 percent if you are a student of color. To compound matters, a high school education is no longer the baseline required for many jobs; in fact, most jobs that enable what we consider a middle-class livelihood now require some post-secondary training, and in many cases, a college degree.

The economic cost of this dysfunctional system, including lost wages, welfare support systems, additional detention facilities, and other programs, runs in the billions of dollars every year. The good news is that addressing this problem should fundamentally not be about funding. In 2010, the United States spent $11,826 per full-time-equivalent (FTE) student on elementary education, 39 percent higher than the OECD average and ranked in the top five. At the postsecondary level, US expenditures per FTE student were $25,576, almost twice as high as the OECD average and ranked number one. Instead of funding proposals, we need a set of common-sense, systematic changes that will improve our approach from the ground up.

TEACHERS MATTER

There is a wide body of anecdotal and structured research that reaches one central conclusion: quality education is all about quality teaching. Teachers are not only the transmitters of information, they are the mentors, motivators, and inspiration leaders for our students. Unfortunately, our system, taken in total, does not adequately reward quality teaching, and the system fails to remove those who just aren't good at their craft. We must pay meaningfully more for quality teaching, and correspondingly, stop paying for poor teaching.

To do that, we have to put in place systems that systematically and fairly evaluate teachers just as we evaluate other professionals in any job. This is just good common sense. We must recognize that seniority and tenure are valued but do not necessarily equal quality teaching and that teachers' rights cannot and must not get in the way of students' rights to a superior classroom experience. Until teachers, administrators, and legislators are willing to address this fundamental issue, no amount of education reform will affect the outcome.

PUTTING IN THE HOURS

The truth today is that most students are not sufficiently challenged academically during the primary and secondary school years, especially in our public education systems. In the anatomy of an average school day, students spend roughly half their time on core academic classes (math, science, social studies, and humanities). Once you factor in school days that average seven hours a day (and fewer on early dismissal days) and the lengthy summer vacation, our students spend less time on primary subjects than students in high-achieving systems. The fine arts and athletics are an important component of educating the "whole child," so this is not a proposal to cut back in these areas. It is a proposal to extend the school day by an hour with all of that time dedicated to core studies. The school year should also be two to three weeks longer to enable deeper learning in important areas. While kids are groaning in the background, they would thrive in, even enjoy, this time if engaged with quality teachers and mentors.

Of course, there are other ways to extend the learning experience and increase the amount of "time on task" for our students. These include after-school and summer programs, either in school locations or through community organizations like Boys and Girls Clubs, YMCAs, and local camps and community centers. Teachers working outside of the school, trained mentors, and volunteers can all play a valuable role in helping students learn away from their regular classroom environment in a way that is not just "more school." The importance of connecting kids with positive mentors who can shape their perspectives on learning cannot be overstated, in particular in communities where parental and family role models are less present. All of this requires school districts to partner with other government and nonprofit agencies in a new way, but the value in terms of educational advancement and safe, social development for students is well worth the effort.

WHERE STUDENTS NEED US MOST

Quality teaching and classroom hours can and must help all levels of the system, but we need a special level of focus on three key age groups: pre-K, middle school, and post-secondary skills programs. By age four, many of the sixteen million children that live in poverty in the United States are already up to eighteen months behind developmentally, a troubling number when you consider that their brains will be 90 percent formed by the time they are five years old. With limited access to preschool and often a difficult learning environment at home, these children require special attention from our government agencies and from private, nonprofit groups.

The next critical point in educating our children is the middle school years. These are years of dramatic changes for students, physically, mentally, and emotionally, and they are also the years that cement their trajectory into high school. An important element of working with these kids is having the courage and ability to teach them essential life skills about healthy habits, including nutrition, substance abuse, and sex education. It is essential to equip our students to deal with today's social realities, and this can be done in public schools in an appropriate way that doesn't tread on religious or other individual rights. If qualified, motivated students can be delivered into the ninth and tenth grades, the odds of successful graduation and post-secondary education increase dramatically.

The final sector in our education system that needs additional support is the community college system and related educational institutions that provide trade training and two-year associate degrees. As a high school diploma becomes insufficient for employment in living-wage-level jobs, the need for basic job skills education increases dramatically and this instruction must be both flexible in its delivery and fundamentally different than a four-year degree. There are a number of interesting new projects in this area, many of which involve partnerships between schools and businesses to create curricula that meet local needs. Some have called this the six-year high school degree that leads to a fulfilling career. We must find ways to re-invigorate this mid-tier, post-secondary system and related training programs that reach a similar audience.

TECHNOLOGY AS A TOOL AND OPPORTUNITY

For some, there is the hope that better technology will improve our schools and the performance of our students. Unfortunately, this is sometimes viewed as a silver bullet where simply spending more money to upgrade school infrastructure will somehow improve classroom performance. The reality is that technology can and should be a part of the solution, but it must be viewed as a means to an end—a tool to enable better teaching. At all levels, technology can be used to deliver high quality, lecture-type instruction, freeing teachers to use more classroom time to teach real applications of the concepts and help students apply their learning. At the post-secondary level, distance learning opens up significant possibilities for all types of education and training without requiring daily classroom attendance. This concept could be particularly valuable for those going to school part-time or trying to improve their trade skills without going to a four-year institution.

At the same time, STEM curricula (science, technology, engineering, and math) offer an area of opportunity for all students. The demand for STEM-educated students, in particular given the evolving nature of the US economy, is only going to increase, and major employers like Microsoft, Google, IBM, and others have thousands of jobs available that they are unable to fill. While easing immigration rules can address some of their needs in the short term, the longer-term solution is to fill these jobs with qualified, local students. Note that not all of these positions require four-year degrees or graduate degrees. Many of them are in related fields that demand technical aptitude but perhaps only an associate degree. Either way, this is an opportunity to provide life-long employment that has a tremendous multiplier effect in the economy.

TRIAL BY FIRE: TAKING IT TO THREE HUNDRED

As this discussion of education reform makes clear, implementing a thirty-page plan involves tremendous scope and scale. Taking this to the next level of detail, the 300-page plan expands that challenge dramatically. Ironically, our Xbox experience demonstrated that this final level of strategic planning is really not strategic at all. It is filled with specific tactics and implementation techniques for bringing the three- and thirty-pagers to life. At some intellectual level, the skills and tools we utilized for Xenon all seemed pretty obvious and straightforward—but their application was deceptively difficult.

The challenge for organizations, whether they are in business or in the civic sector, is ensuring that these specifics are well executed. When the pressures of time, resource scarcity, and the organizational physics of people working together (or not) are added, many products and initiatives go awry in the execution phase. New Coke, the Chevrolet Vega, Apple's Newton, IBM's PCJr., and Microsoft's Zune (yes, I led that one) all come to mind as examples of products that were badly executed, mistimed, or both. These types of failures are hardly limited to the business world—there are a number of excellent civic examples as well. Two projects, one in Boston, the other in Seattle, illustrate what happens when strategy meets poor execution.

THE BIG DIG AND THE SEQUEL

During the first half of my career at Microsoft, I traveled to Boston about once a year for various meetings, conventions, and other functions. When my daughter enrolled in Boston College recently and I joined a board of directors that meets regularly in Boston, I once again began visiting the home of the Red Sox, Celtics, Patriots, and Bruins with some regularity. What surprised me is how much more I enjoyed the city during my more recent visits.

I'm sure some of this has to do with the purpose of my meetings and more time spent in the city as a tourist rather than as a visiting businessman. But Boston has evolved in the interim with more green spaces, better traffic (although still with its challenges), and a skyline that is quite impressive. So what has changed? To my uneducated, West Coast mind, the completion of the Big Dig stands out as something that both plagued and then transformed Boston.

The original concept for this project was to redesign several roadways that were arterial clogs in the transportation system and eyesores across the waterfront by burying them underground in a series of tunnels. This plan went through a number of phases, starts, and stops beginning in the 1980s, followed by the first groundbreaking in 1991. Whether the final strategy approved was perfect or even directionally correct is a subject for Bostonians to argue, but there is no doubt that the implementation on that strategy was an unmitigated disaster.

The tale of the numbers says it all: originally scheduled to be completed in 1998, the project was finally completed in 2007. Even adjusting for inflation (which is cheating to some degree because the delays increased the cost), the project had a 190 percent cost overrun, not including the additional financing costs that are still being incurred. Some estimates indicate it will not be fully paid off until after 2030. Leaks, design issues, criminal indictments, and settlements of civil lawsuits also affected the Dig. The outcome is undeniably better than the situation prior to the project, but the effort was grossly mismanaged. Either Boston leaders missed the memo on the need for detailed specifications or the equivalent of a 300-page plan was poorly executed.

Ironically, the city of Seattle seems to be on course to repeat this same mistake. Like Boston, the Seattle waterfront includes an elevated highway, State Route 99, which must be replaced due to earthquake damage. This route regularly becomes a parking lot during rush hour, blocks the skyline, and prevents easy access to the waterfront. The city and state wrangled for a number of years before agreeing on a strategy for replacing the so-called Alaskan Way Viaduct, finally settling on a financial and structural plan after several lawsuits, citizens' initiatives, and some mayoral temper tantrums. Ironically, the final solution involved digging a tunnel under and through downtown Seattle.

Right on cue, the project got off to a difficult start. The giant tunnel-boring machine required to create the tubes for traffic suddenly stopped working. In part, this was caused by large metal pipes left in the dig zone, following a process to collect core samples of the soil. The presence of these pipes was not mysterious; the process for evaluating the tunnel put them there. The stalled digging and repairs required to the boring machine have created ancillary problems with ground instability, water management, and other issues. The city, the state, the contractor, and several other groups involved are pointing fingers at one another, and the implementation treadmill leading to missed dates and escalating costs is off and running.

I suppose one lesson here is that tunnels are complicated, but that, of course, is not the point. These civic examples amplify the hard lessons we learned taking Xbox to market and the importance of specific tactics and day-to-day skill sets. The original Xbox had issues with everything from complaints that the DVD drives scratched disks to controllers that were too large for your hands to noisy fans that made movies difficult to watch. While the 3P Framework helped us improve our performance with Xbox 360, we still had meaningful operational challenges, including the $1 billion red rings write-off and warranty extension.

In the end, even if you have an excellent strategy, or even just a reasonable strategy that is well understood, the leadership team must shift its focus from strategy development to project execution and apply the same level of diligence to ensure that the plan is implemented successfully. In a civic context, we cannot sit back and assume that others will take care of the details. The "silenced majority" that occupies the middle ground on most issues must stand up and vocally assert its power to adopt and implement practical proposals for change. Personal, parochial interests must be set aside in favor of what is required for the good of the country as a whole. Courage, accountability, sacrifice, and commitment are the necessary characteristics for all of us.

> In a civic context, we cannot sit back and assume that others will take care of the details. The "silenced majority" that occupies the middle ground on most issues must stand up and vocally assert its power to adopt and implement practical proposals for change.

Whether you are an individual, small business owner, local non-profit board member, city council representative, CEO of a major corporation, or president of the world's most important democracy, the 3P Framework can provide strategic direction and guidance, but that is only part of the story.

XBOX LESSON NUMBER FOUR

Effective implementation and ultimate success is about the details embodied in a thirty- and 300-pager and your commitment to seeing things through.

12

THE PEOPLE PRINCIPLE

As we moved from the 3/30/300 process into day-to-day plan implementation, J Allard and I debated whether there should be one more P—the critical element of people. Strong leaders at all levels of the organization or civic initiative are absolutely essential to drive strategic change, particularly in complex situations. And as the process advances from strategy to tactics and implementation, the importance of great team members is also magnified. In many respects, people are the X-factor that can turn a merely good strategy into a great business, or conversely can transform a truly great idea into an operational failure.

Even though the Xbox team was often dysfunctional early in its formation, the talent level was always quite high, providing a safety net for other shortcomings. Ultimately, proactive leadership, the 3P Framework efforts, and time together on task, shaped us into a strong, highly skilled team. In contrast, many of our government organizations suffer from a shortcoming of great people, in large part reflecting in Charles Roscovitch's concerns about the electoral process. The Simpson-Bowles Commission's demise demonstrates that without

> In many respects, people are the X-factor that can turn a merely good strategy into a great business, or conversely can transform a truly great idea into an operational failure.

the right people in the right positions at the right time, no amount of framework creation or good planning will lead to constructive outcomes. There are no foolproof approaches to team development and management, but great leaders find a way to attract the right people—and the right people form great teams—and great teams win.

> There are no foolproof approaches to team development and management, but great leaders find a way to attract the right people—and the right people form great teams —and great teams win.

HEADS ON MOUNT RUSHMORE

From 1927 to 1941, Gutzon Borglum and over 400 workers carved the faces of four famous American leaders into the granite of Mount Rushmore. Originally designed to drive tourism in the Dakotas, the monument enshrines four presidents because of their critical role in creating, preserving, and growing the United States. Whether they were the greatest presidents during America's first 150 years or not, Washington, Jefferson, Lincoln, and Roosevelt were all great leaders in their time.

In today's leadership void, it is important to ask the hypothetical question: "Whom would we add to Mount Rushmore now?" A strong case can be made for Franklin Roosevelt, given his role in leading us through the Great Depression and Second World War, and I suspect John F. Kennedy would get some votes, along with Ronald Reagan. With due respect to these presidents and an impressive list of senators and representatives, I don't see any real candidates from government over the past fifty years. Instead, my personal vote would go to Martin Luther King Jr. for his role in leading the Civil Rights Movement in the 1950s and 60s. While his dream is still not a reality, he led with vision and clarity and changed American society forever for the better. Given the crisis of competence we have in government today, we need many more leaders like him.

The history of Xbox reinforces the critical role leaders play in driving transformational change. To return to our construction analogy, if purpose, principles, and priorities define the shape and form of the building, it takes a great architect and contractor to complete construction. Real leadership is the art of working through others to turn the possible into reality, overcoming all of the obstacles and challenges along the way. Providing this level of guidance and mentorship happens every day in small, medium, and large doses. And not everyone has to be "Rushmore-worthy" in the scale and scope of what they do—some leaders will run major divisions while others will lead a small team on a specific product. Still others will lead a local town council, community committee, or nonprofit board. All contribute in their own ways to the broader solutions laid out in a strategic framework.

I won't presume to define specific requirements for great leadership—there is no single recipe that works even most of the time—but there are important attributes to consider. Great leaders are the metaphorical equivalent of the Avengers: each has to understand his or her "superpowers" and match their individual skills to the issues at hand. Some leaders have the brains of Iron Man, others bring the virtue and commitment of Captain America, while still others use the stealth of Black Widow. The important point is that they understand and appreciate their strengths and weaknesses and lead appropriately. Sometimes this means only taking on challenges that require their unique skills, while in other situations it means modifying their leadership style to match the circumstances.

Comparing Dwight Eisenhower and George Patton, two prominent and successful World War II generals, brings this concept into sharp relief. Eisenhower's job was to forge a strong partnership with our European allies during World War II, negotiate roles and responsibilities that involved everyone appropriately, and orchestrate across multiple arms of the military within the United States. He needed to be both a statesman as well as the military leader responsible for success in Europe. Patton, on the other hand, was uniquely qualified to rally the troops, drive them hard, and push through any obstacles that got in his way, including the bureaucratic and diplomatic niceties. He was the consummate field commander who fought hard for the home team without really being a team player. Both Eisenhower and Patton were great leaders, and both would likely have failed if required to swap roles. In the end, only one of them was qualified to be president of the United States.

Beyond their individual attributes, strong leaders know how to tap into the talents of others, in particular to fill gaps in their own skill set. The English Old Testament scholar H. Wheeler Robinson once said that "the penalty of leadership is loneliness," and I suspect an entire choir could be created from those who have experienced the loneliness of making difficult, even life-and-death decisions. Successful leaders are actually those who find a way to surround themselves with strong, capable people, leverage their talents to establish and execute on strategy, and make those difficult decisions.

Upon being elected president, Abraham Lincoln immediately set to work forming his cabinet from the very individuals whom he'd campaigned against during the Republican Party nomination process. This certainly unified the Party behind his presidency, but his ongoing motivation was to benefit from the skills, ideas, and intellectual engagement of those most qualified. Even though working with his former rivals made his cabinet dysfunctional in many traditional respects, he was brilliant at extracting the best from each member and molding that into his own policies and strategies. He, of all presidents, experienced the loneliness of making difficult decisions, but his legacy on Mount Rushmore was built on the support and advice of lesser-known but still great leaders.

If each group has a leader and a set of lieutenants, it also has individual members—people who need to follow the leadership team to be successful. Consequently, those at the top of the pyramid need to embody certain personal characteristics that attract others to their organization. Charisma, fortitude, compassion, integrity, and empathy fall into this category of attributes. These can be mixed in various proportions to suit the situation and the leader, but in the end, they add up to one important concept: people must respect those that they follow. As different as they were personally, Eisenhower and Patton demanded and commanded the respect of their troops. Their success was not about whether people "liked" them—leadership is not always related to likeability. Respect is the foundation on which most leaders build their influence and ability to drive teams successfully. Every leader needs to remember that respect is very difficult to build and remarkably easy to lose.

> Respect is the foundation on which most leaders build their influence and ability to drive teams successfully. Every leader needs to remember that respect is very difficult to build and remarkably easy to lose.

IT'S A TEAM SPORT

The people equation, of course, does not end with the leader or even the organization's broader leadership group. Great leaders do more than provide direction: they ensure that the right individuals are added to the project both in terms of their functional skills as well as their fit within the group. In fact, if you ask a coach how championships are won, he will tell you that they involve some combination of leadership, team chemistry, and great individual skills.

In building a 3P Framework, strong leaders consider the specific skill sets they will need relative to the top five priorities in their plan. Like any good professional sports general manager, they determine their key skill positions, evaluate the talent that is available internally and externally, and hire for specific roles to match. When building a team from scratch, the challenge is finding pools of talent, figuring out which pieces to add first, and determining how to match each piece to the others that become available. For existing organizations, matching the team to a new set of strategic initiatives may require only a small number of changes in people or minor adjustments to their current roles and responsibilities. On the other hand, the team may need to be reshaped in a dramatic way.

When I took over the Windows Mobile Phone effort in 2006, I allowed the existing team to wrestle with a set of strategic problems they were ill equipped to solve. I let them continue their work for almost a year before conceding that major changes were needed. We finally developed a new approach that required many different skill sets and replaced roughly 60 percent of the managers across the team. The nine-month leeway that I gave the original team proved expensive relative to our emerging competition with Apple and Google, and I learned the hard way that it is better to be decisive when making changes rather than allowing the old organization and people to linger.

Once the core skill positions are evaluated and filled, shaping the rest of the team and developing a defined culture is a longer-range project. In the Xbox example, it took almost four years to build a culture of consistently strong teamwork, and even then, it was never a truly harmonious family. The personnel and team chemistry aspects of this, naturally, need to be grounded in the principles established earlier in the strategy, but they also are strongly influenced by the managers and skill-position players involved. Actions always speak louder than words, so culture must reflect the way leaders conduct themselves and vice versa. There is no single culture that works well all of the time. I've seen highly collegial cultures succeed as well as those that would be better described as benevolent dictatorships. If you compare two companies like Google and Apple, you'd find cultures that are vastly different—and yet they are both successful in the consumer technology space.

When filling in the more general-purpose roles, an organization should hire for overall talent and potential and then work aggressively to instill the right habits in the people once they are on board. This approach provides more flexibility in terms of moving people around the organization and also creates an environment where people are constantly learning, which increases retention and job satisfaction. In most cases, people are at least equally motivated by the amount they are learning and their interest in the task at hand as they are with the amount of money you are paying them. The goal is to build what someone once called a "supply chain of human capital": a motivated group of employees who are ready to pursue a 3P Framework with vigor and energy.

CIVIC ENGINEERS

Orchestrating a skilled set of individuals into a cohesive team is more challenging in civic situations. These organizations as a whole have different decision-making process and structure than most businesses. As the task moves from the general strategy to the core decisions, competing interests create serious side currents for leaders and teams. Whether it is the collegial attitude that drives most nonprofits or the politics of electioneering that rules many political organizations, making concrete decisions on controversial topics is just more difficult in the civic arena. Moreover, the talent pool is constrained to some degree by the need for individuals to be connected to the cause in some way, and salaries and benefits are generally lower than in the for-profit world. The net result is a definite shortage of what I call "civic engineers," qualified, committed people who focus on doing the right thing for the community at large.

As a member of both local and national nonprofit boards, I've experienced the dynamics that occur in civic organizations between staff, executive directors/CEOs, and their boards. I've actively participated in these conversations as a board member and as board chair at the local and national levels. And while there are plenty of dysfunctional relationships in these organizations, there is nothing structural that prevents leaders from driving strategic change. I've watched two strong nonprofit CEOs at the USOC and Boys and Girls Clubs of America implement dramatic change at both the local and national levels, using many of the tools and techniques discussed in the 3P Framework (even if they didn't think of it that way). Importantly, they had the backing of experienced, effective boards who supported and enabled the process. The equivalent of a thirty-pager is alive and well in these types of organizations.

The situation is more complicated and less encouraging in government organizations. These institutions will never operate the same way as businesses or even nonprofits, and no amount of strategy work is going to change that. By definition, the leadership changes with great regularity, and those elected are presented with an odd combination of lifelong government officials, lobbyists, consultants, and an ever-shifting mix of Democrats and Republicans across the executive and legislative branches.

At the national level, each legislator gets to hire individual staff; government administrators develop their careers within their departmental or functional areas of expertise; and the president has his team of cabinet members, advisors, and, in the current administration, policy czars. To govern effectively, this unruly collection of individuals has to work together on a regular basis to drive government policy. The people, process, and outcomes, not surprisingly, are often not ideal. The 3P Framework can be an early and effective tool to help these teams focus on what is important and work better together, but it is only one piece of the puzzle. We need more civic engineers willing to commit their time and talents at all levels of government to transform these organizations to work more effectively. How we bring American level entrepreneurship to bear on government management processes requires a thirty-page plan of its own.

THE UNKNOWNS

We tend to assume that leadership, whether in government or in the private sector, is associated with those in positions of power or explicit influence. Another path to change revolves around those who are not well known, famous, or occupying high positions. Nevertheless, they are people with the ability to take on big issues and have great impact. Passionate individuals on a mission can form a very powerful force when viewed collectively. Unless you happen to be engaged in their specific fields of expertise, I bet few readers will recognize Ha

Partovi, Jabe Blumenthal, or Gerald Chertavian, but they are just a few examples of individuals driving the forces of change.

Hadi Partovi was a founder or part of the founding team for a number of successful start-up companies, including TellMe (which Microsoft bought) and iLike (which MySpace bought). He was also an investor or early advisor to numerous start-ups, including Facebook, Dropbox, and Airbnb, and he worked at Microsoft several times during his career. He is definitely a talented entrepreneur who understands technology and building businesses.

Recently, he turned his attention to another endeavor—addressing the sad state of technology education in our public schools, with particular emphasis on teaching computer science and the art of writing code. He and his brother, Ali, have formed an organization called Code.org, which is on a mission to bring computer science classes to every K-12 public school in the United States. In the process, they hope to change the very definition of math and science curricula and increase the number of women and students of color in this twenty-first century field. Starting with a single program, called The Hour of Code, they have reached tens of millions of students worldwide, and one in every three students in the United States. The Partovis are helping to transform our education system.

Jabe Blumenthal is another Microsoft alum, although his current line of work has nothing to do with his groundbreaking efforts designing products like Excel and Works. Jabe left Microsoft in 1994 to teach mathematics and physics at Lakeside High School in Seattle, where he eventually became the head of the science department. Since leaving Lakeside in 2003, he has increased his involvement in environmental efforts with an emphasis on what I would call "solution-oriented environmentalism." Jabe is definitely no shrinking violet about the damage we are doing to our ecosystems, and he utilizes his science and business backgrounds to look for practical solutions. He is open to exploring coalitions with organizations that traditionally have not worked well together, to demonstrate that we can power our society, grow our economy, and protect our environment all at the same time, rather than make some false choice between these things. Jabe is a progressive leader for change in an area where cooperation and thoughtful leadership are desperately needed.

Gerald Chertavian started his professional career in banking on Wall Street, eventually migrating to a marketing position in a financial institution in London. He co-founded a company called Conduit Communications in 1993, which he grew significantly and sold six years later. At that point, he shifted his focus from success to significance with the founding of Year Up, a year-long education and professional job-training program for urban young adults.

Year Up includes six months of structured career and skills education for students with high school degrees or GEDs who are unlikely to pursue a four-year program. Students then participate in a six-month internship with local companies with the goal of landing living-wage employment when they graduate at the end of the year. Year Up has expanded from its start-up in Boston to a total of fourteen cities and has trained over 10,000 young adults. Gerald's leadership is changing the way we think about job training, skills development, and mentorship.

It is no accident that I highlighted Hadi, Jabe, and Gerald; they are innovators having positive impact across the range of the five priorities established in the American three-pager. And there are thousands of individuals like them, well known in their own areas and profession-al communities but unknown in the broad context of the fight face. To win that fight, we need to reward these civic engineers and their entrepreneurial efforts by fixing many of the structural issues they experience, creating an infrastructure of opportunity, and using common-sense solutions to change the course of our country.

THE PROPOSAL

The "People Principle" that J Allard and I debated is certainly about finding individuals willing to lead, but it is equally about everyone on the team standing up and being counted to make a difference. I am generally an optimist about most challenges, and I'm certainly inspired by the work of great historic leaders and my contemporary associates who are committing their lives to civic causes. But sadly, the guiding light for many of our leaders, especially at the national level, is not what is right for the country. Instead, they are guided by what helps them get re-elected. In the words of Michael Bloomberg, "There's something more important than getting elected, and that's standing up and saying what you think is right."

We don't need Democrats or Republicans, Tea Parties or Socialists, Liberals or Conservatives. We need statesmen and stateswomen who will put the country's interests in front of their own. We need independent thinkers who focus on solving real issues, building their efforts on a foundation of purpose, principles, and priorities, creating strategies that lead to common-sense solutions. We also need the silent majority of individuals who represent the broad middle ground of American thought to stand up and be counted.

> We need independent thinkers who focus on solving real issues, building their efforts on a foundation of purpose, principles, and priorities, creating strategies that lead to common-sense solutions.

Who will rise up to take on our challenges? Who will truly do the right thing? Who will stand at the base of Mount Rushmore and aspire to do more?

To my generation and my peers, I present the following proposition: our country has a rich history, tremendous resources, and remarkable potential. But we are letting all of that slip away, and on our current course and speed, we will leave only deeper challenges for our children and their children. It's time for the civic engineers amongst us to saddle up and be counted. I hope you will join Charles Roscovitch and me in tackling the challenges ahead. Now is the time, these are the issues; we need citizens to stand up, demand change, and return us to a position of strength and prosperity.

A RETURN TO COMMON SENSE

When all of the rules, processes, and frameworks have been explained, when all of the stories and anecdotes have been cleverly told, when opinions and points of view have been offered, we are left with two words: "So what?" Perhaps a bit barren and naked, but very real.

And my response, will be equally blunt and explicit:

- *Get educated:* civic issues are too important to leave to others.
- *Get vocal:* constructive debate motivates others and drives change.
- *Get involved:* pick a cause, a policy issue, a candidate—and make sure you vote.

This is what it means to become a civic engineer. Like other forms of engineering, this discipline requires focus, effort, diligence, and commitment. Unlike the more formal degree programs, it is not an exclusive club. In fact, rather than requiring years of study, advanced diplomas, and a certain love for geekdom, civic engineering is the most democratic of clubs, requiring only that we live up to our duties as citizens and apply our common sense.

> In fact, rather than requiring years of study, advanced diplomas, and a certain love for geekdom, civic engineering is the most democratic of clubs, requiring only that we live up to our duties as citizens and apply our common sense.

When you take a new job or go to work for a new company, getting educated, vocal, and involved are things that come naturally. You learn the company's products, your role in bringing them to life, and the goals that define success. By definition, you get engaged in the specific tasks that are important for your job and become a part of the day-to-day fabric of the organization. And when provided the opportunity, successful employees have strong opinions about what is correct or incorrect about a certain course of action. The "so what" of *Xbox Revisited* proposes (and indeed demands) that we apply these same concepts to civic engagement. As civic engineers, we can apply the same 3P Framework that worked so well for the Xbox to the civic issues that matter to us most. Think of the momentum and progress we could generate if each of us used our common-sense instincts to improve the communities around us.

THE CIVIC ENGINEERING CURRICULUM

I was at a bar mitzvah party recently and ended up in a discussion with a Frenchman and a Georgian (the country, not the state) about the fate of Eastern Europe in the face of Vladimir Putin's invasion of the Ukraine. We had an educated, vocal, and involved conversation that was highly enjoyable and perhaps shifted each of our points of view. I'm sure it wasn't felt in Kiev, nor were there any great conclusions, but these conversations are the atomic elements of a well-functioning society that challenges itself to be better. They are the first steps in a civic process that drives change.

In some ways, getting educated on civic issues has never been easier. Our founding fathers barely had a printing press—we have access to TV, radio, newspapers, Internet news sites, blogs, and more rudimentary but ubiquitous communications tools like Twitter and

Facebook. Unfortunately, the surplus of media outlets has actually made getting educated on civic issues more difficult. Sorting through the wheat from the chaff is challenging, editorial integrity is often AWOL, and the most outrageous voices in the blogosphere get the most attention. And most importantly, the political extremes take advantage of this maelstrom of information to promulgate their version of the truth.

A real curriculum for pragmatic civic engineers requires going back to some basics: just like any college class, there is a set of books and papers that must be read. While this list is not exhaustive, it provides a good foundation of relevant subject matter—importantly, these readings are all from highly credible sources who certainly have a point of view but are appropriately researched and editorially managed:

1. ***The Penguin Guide to the United States Constitution:*** I know it sounds old fashioned, but reading the documents that shaped our country is a core element in understanding how citizens must participate. Richard Beeman's book also provides interesting annotations of the Declaration of Independence and selections from the Federalist Papers.

2. ***USA, Inc.: A Basic Summary of America's Financial Statements:*** Like any report on the financial condition of a company, Mary Meeker's analysis of the finances of the United States explores the shaky foundation on which we currently stand.

3. ***The Moment of Truth: Report of the National Commission on Fiscal Responsibility and Reform:*** In addition to painting a policy portrait for what must be done, the so-called Simpson-Bowles report

demonstrates that pragmatic, common-sense solutions are there to be found.

4. ***The Price of Politics:*** Bob Woodward's book chronicling the budget debates during the Obama administration provides a detailed, insider's view of the dysfunction in Washington, DC. I found it difficult to finish—not because it was poorly written but because it was so frustrating.

5. ***The Centrist Manifesto:*** Like most people, I'd never heard of Charles Wheelan until someone pointed me to his book proposing a platform for change centered literally on the fulcrum of the political spectrum. This policy approach is common sense personified, and the pathway to change is unique and compelling.

In addition to these core readings, a subscription to *The Week* is in order. While not an in-depth publication, it covers a broad swath of policy issues weekly and does so by presenting all sides of the issue. The magazine and accompanying website provide extensive references and links to more complete articles on each topic and act as a clearinghouse for the full spectrum of ideas. Regardless of the specific books and publications selected, the number-one requirement is finding sources with editorial integrity and an independent, well-researched point of view.

LET'S PARTY

Getting vocal and involved require both more individual choices and more collective action. Civic engineering demands real passion and commitment, so every citizen has to evaluate various causes and issues to determine their particular area of focus. For some, this will be an extension or expansion of work they already do—certainly this was the case for my deep and broad commitment to the Boys and Girls Clubs of America, where I began as a volunteer basketball coach at a local club. For others, this will require research and thought, both to find areas of passion and then to vet various organizations that are involved. The only statement I can make with certainty is that we all share one civic organization, namely our government, and we all have an obligation to get involved in that important set of institutions. As Charles Wheelan says, paraphrasing Edmund Burke, "All that is necessary for bad governance is that sensible, well-intentioned people choose not to engage in the process."

> "All that is necessary for bad governance is that sensible, well-intentioned people choose not to engage in the process."

America is a representative democracy predicated on the idea that if the people don't like the decisions being made, they can replace their representatives. Unfortunately, this portion of the democratic process is failing, in large part because of gerrymandering, election-funding calculus, and the dearth of quality candidates. The extremes of the political spectrum on both the conservative and liberal sides are exceptionally well funded and organized, certainly more so than the silent majority in the middle. Presumably, they also feel as if they have more at stake and are more committed to their cause. As a result, the civic agenda is currently being held hostage by a small group of people polarizing every debate into a win-lose discussion or alternatively, gridlock.

Time and time again, our elected officials have taken the easy path—the path that leads them around issues; the path that divides them along ideological lines; the path that panders to special interests;

the path that postpones problems for someone else to manage; the path that is high on brinkmanship and low on bipartisanship; the path that goes nowhere quickly.

This failure of leadership runs through local, state, and federal governments and in particular has characterized the actions of our presidents, our representatives, and our senators, as well as those running for office for at least a decade. Independent of whether I like or dislike their viewpoints on specific issues, they have failed as leaders, they have failed to put the country's best interests in the forefront, they have failed to find the appropriate middle ground, and there must be consequences for that failure.

To utilize our representative democratic process effectively, the independent centrists in our country need to organize into an active, powerful force that can energize the silent majority to demand change. Creating a new center of gravity requires engagement from people who have generally been on the sidelines of civic debate, and that includes people like me. These leaders may or may not be candidates for office, but they can certainly provide the resources and organizational skills to bring American political thought back into the mainstream.

Instead of settling for the "better of two evils," which is the way many elections feel today, this group needs to command the attention of candidates and pull them back to the appropriate common-sense positions. Voters should have difficult choices, but choices that involve picking the best of the mainstream rather than the least extreme of the outliers. This is particularly true in primary elections where centrist candidates have been defeated by fringe candidates who are well funded and get out their vote in generally poorly attended elections. And the reality is that district partitioning has made the primary election the de facto final vote in many communities.

The extreme form of this constituent activism is to form a new, centrist political group. As an example, instead of debating whether the Tea Party or the RINOs (so called Republicans in Name Only) control the Republican Party, why not just create a new party? For those that believe in returning to common sense, the challenge becomes forming a coalition of existing independents, financially conservative Democrats, and socially moderate Republicans that can either force their respective parties back to the center or create their own party.

To do this effectively, a small group of people must craft a policy platform to serve as a manifesto. This platform should start with a 3P Framework process, and whether or not it reaches the same conclusions outlined in the American three-pager, it needs to lay out those core policies in an easy-to-digest format with clear purpose, concrete principles, and disciplined priorities. The group will need charismatic leaders capable of generating personal respect from a broad cross section of America and rallying potential members to the cause. And that cause requires a grassroots collection of civic engineers to provide the practical, day-to-day ideas that will drive success.

There are already policy groups like the Bipartisan Policy Center attempting to bring centrists together at a policy level, and although they've met with mixed success, the effort is important. The Centrist Project is another organization pursuing centrist ideals but with a different focus. Based on Charles Wheelan's *Centrist Manifesto*, their current goal is to focus on electing five to six independent centrists to the Senate, recognizing that this group would be the "swing vote" on any policy debates between the Democrats and the Republicans. Presumably, this would be the cornerstone for attracting other moderates from both parties with the ultimate goal to present a third party to voters on a broader basis.

Frankly, even for a self-aware idealist like me, forming a new party sounds exceptionally naïve and strains the chains of credibility. But fractious, difficult times create the opportunity for real change. It is easy to forget that the Republican Party was formed in 1854 as a re-combination of elements of the Whig Party and "free-soil" Democrats in response to legislative struggles over the future of slavery. Only six years later, Abraham Lincoln was elected president as a Republican. We need the modern equivalent of those pioneering civic engineers of the nineteenth century if we are going change the direction of our country.

THE FINAL WORD

A few years ago, I had the honor to give a short talk at the baccalaureate celebration for my daughter's high school. Having your graduating daughter introduce you to speak is one of life's special moments, certainly one that was emotional enough to make even me pause before beginning my speech. Every graduating senior in that audience had been asked the same set of questions—"Where are you going to school?" "What's your major?" "Do you know what you want to do after school?"—as if having a life plan was a graduation requirement. As the guy whose plan thirty-four years ago was to go to law school and become a US senator, I can vouch for the fact that plans are nice but life has a habit of intervening.

When I left Microsoft after twenty-two years, I felt much like all of those high school seniors at the baccalaureate. Everyone kept asking me, "What is your plan?" and "What are you going to do next?" As I reflected on those darkest of days in 2001 that changed my life and contemplated the path forward, I realized my next steps would lead to a second career in civic engineering. America is at a crossroads, one of those pivotal points in history that will determine the trajectory of our future. Those challenging days and my cross-country sojourn also showed me the strength and character of our country and its citizens. Now a decade later, I remain convinced we can conquer the most complex of challenges if properly mobilized.

Which brings us back to where we started and the central point of *Xbox Revisited*. If we want to continue to be the land of opportunity and home of the free and brave, we must have a better plan for investing in that future. The 3P Framework that I learned through our Xbox odyssey is a tool to prepare that plan, to establish our purpose, to set our principles, and to choose our priorities. Of course, we desperately need a few Eisenhowers, Trumans, Roosevelts (both of them), and several Lincolns to guide us. In combination with concepts like 3/30/300 and the leadership of thousands of Mount Rushmore-capable civic engineers, we can build a practical strategy that will provide a powerful legacy for future generations. If we proceed with faith, act with perseverance, and take advantage of opportunities—if we *return to common sense*—we can transform America.

ACKNOWLEDGMENTS

When I began this project, I really started writing for me. Whether because of a "midlife crisis," misplaced ego, or need to fulfill a childhood ambition, much of what I've written in this book has been brewing inside of me for some time. Patriotism, fiscal conservatism, social moderation, constructive compromise, and rational simplicity have all been a part of my life for as long as I can remember, and I've been the most confused, unhappy, and dysfunctional when I've lost connection with those roots. Being raised in a midwest, Germanic family may sound boring, but I'm thankful every day for the seeds my family sowed. So in many ways, this was an opportunity for me to reconnect with my roots, to reestablish in my mind the foundations of my beliefs. To my mom and dad, I say simply, "I love you."

The fact that *Xbox Revisited* is now a reality has a great deal to do with the support and guidance I've received from friends, family, co-workers, and a whole group of people I met through the writing and publishing process. They say that it "takes a village," and that has never been truer than the creation of this book. Since I am an absent-minded professor at times, I know I will forget to thank someone important. Please chalk that up to my own issues rather than lack of gratitude. So with great humility and deep thanks, I offer the following:

To Pauline, Phillip, Nicoline, and Madeline: the most important loves come first.

To Team Xbox: the journey was the reward, and I was proud and privileged to travel with you.

To Bill, Steve, Jeff, Pete, and all of Microsoft: I loved every bit of the twenty-two-year opportunity.

To J: your passion and vision set a higher standard and drove all of us to excel

To the Taurus gang: never forget.

To Tina: you taught me to tell stories and inspired me to make this story so much better.

To Pete, Kim, Moshe, Chuck, and Brad: you read the early musings with great patience and ideas.

To Doug and Marland: your inside-the-beltway perspectives and suggestions brought me back to reality.

To Jack and Anne: such wonderful life guides.

To Rick: I am grateful you rejected that 2:00 a.m. email and introduced me to so many helpful people.

To Frank, Steve, and Brad: your support, suggestions, and approvals all made a huge difference.

To John, David, Shane, and Matt: you added the many details that I could not remember.

To Todd, Peter, and Mitch: thanks for keeping me straight on the facts.

To Milli and everyone at Brown Books: I'm grateful that you think authors come first.

To Danelle, Janet, and Derek: I now love editors and revision marks; you made the difference.

To Chris and Gail: your respectful "no thank you" opened doors to the right "yes please."

To Scott, Jabe, Hadi, and Gerald: thanks for providing such inspiring content.

To my brothers, sisters, and their spouses: Sock Boy and baby brother loves you.

To Ashley, Matt, and Leslie: the creativity you supplied filled a big gap in my skill set.

To the Kiawah gang: family is forever; let the traditions live on.

To Charles: faithful companions are difficult to find; let's go for a walk.

Faith, Perseverance, and Serendipity: life lessons to live by.

THE XENON REVISITED THREE-PAGER

Author's Note: The original Xenon three-pager combined purpose and principles as one section of the overall strategy. Based on our experience utilizing and refining the framework, we concluded that these were separate and distinct disciplines that required their own sections. In the revisited version of the Xenon three-pager presented below, this separation of purpose from principles has been applied to the original content to better display how the 3P Framework should be employed. I've also removed small elements of technical jargon and redacted some data for confidentiality purposes. None of the strategy elements (for better or worse) have been edited or modified.

From: Robbie Bach
Cc: BillG, SteveB, JimAl, WPoole, DavidCol, JohnCon
Subject: Part 1 of the 3/30/300 Xenon Trilogy
Date: April 2, 2003 [as edited]

At our recent management team offsite, we decided to build a more comprehensive and integrated planning process across our products and functional areas. In particular, we concluded that while the team was doing an excellent job driving the technical specs for Xenon, they were doing this without enough context or foundation principles against which they could make tradeoffs. We agreed that our Xenon planning process would be built around three documents: a 3-page document focusing on Purpose, Principles, and Priorities (drafting author: RobbieB), a 30-page document that fleshes that out into strategy and product principles (drafting author: JAllard), and a 300-page detailed product and business specification (drafting authors: Xenon Planning Team). We call this our 3/30/300 plan. Our goal is to have all of these documents drafted, reviewed, and "completed" by June 30, 2003. The remainder of this document is dedicated to defining our Xenon Purpose, Principles, and Priorities.

PURPOSE

Microsoft has a broad vision that digital technology is transforming the entertainment world in dramatic ways and this process will accelerate over the next 10 years. As a company, we are investing heavily in Xbox, eHome, MSN, MSTV, Windows, and other areas to position ourselves as a leader in this transformation. Xbox plays a critical role in driving this change within the interactive entertainment area—the arena that is focused on gaming but also includes elements from music, video, and TV. With that in mind, the Xenon project should be based on the following Purpose Statement:

Xenon brings innovative forms of gaming and interactive entertainment to more living rooms than ever before.

The original Xbox focused solely on gaming, and in particular on "hard core" gamers. We optimized all of the specifications to enable developers and producers to create powerful games for the expert gamer. To be successful, Xenon must drive significantly higher volume, and we can't do that only competing in the core gaming space. Consequently, we will produce games that appeal to a wider audience because our research shows that many Xboxes are not allowed into the "living room" or even into the house by some parents, especially mothers. This will include games that some call "casual games" or "games for kids." To further broaden our reach, our purpose for Xenon adds additional forms of interactive entertainment, including music, TV, movies, and every shade of entertainment in between. We will also build on our innovative and fast-growing Xbox Live service. Our goal is to expand on our beachhead with gamers and turn Xbox Live into a diverse entertainment service that a broad demographic will enjoy and value.

PRINCIPLES

To ensure that our decision making is properly grounded and consistent across the team, we've established the following operating principles for the project:

1. *Maximize Return to Investors:* With Xenon, we are crystal clear that the business, taken in total, has to make money, and not just a few hundred million dollars but in the "billions of dollars" range. To do that, we will re-design our platform from end to end, both within development and across sales and marketing. This change in approach requires significant work and coordination across all aspects of the business, including everything from maximizing the attach rate of Xbox Live subscribers to re-designing our packaging so that we can fit more boxes in ocean freight containers and thus reduce shipping costs.

2. *Reach New Customers and Expand the Market:* In addition to transforming the profitability of our products, we also need significantly more volume to

cover the substantial fixed costs in development and marketing associated with a console launch. Sony will have a huge advantage upgrading its existing customers so growing our volume through a dramatic shift in gaming market share seems unlikely. Instead, we will attempt to grow the market, believing that we have a better chance to win over newer, less committed customers. With video games in only 40 percent of US households and far fewer outside the US, this is the right bet to place.

3. ***Optimize for Gaming First, Then Digital Lifestyle:*** One way to grow the market is to expand beyond the core gaming audience with new types of games, while another strategy is to push aggressively into other forms of entertainment, including TV and movies. As a core principle, we must secure our gaming customers first and then expand into other areas of entertainment. Exploring new types of games beyond sports, speed, explosions, fantasy, and guns requires some careful planning because we can't afford to abandon our core audience. We also don't have the creative or development talent for these new types of games, and shifting the culture to value other forms of gaming will take time and effort. The team must secure this part of the plan and then pursue a whole initiative around the "digital lifestyle." This encompasses other forms of entertainment (TV, movies, music, etc.) and will incorporate them into Xbox Live.

4. ***Build a Global Business:*** Our PR notwithstanding, the original Xbox is an English-speaking product. We've done well in North America, the UK, Australia, and most parts of Northern Europe, while our business in Central and Eastern Europe is only "OK." We are performing very poorly in Southern Europe, have little presence in Central and South America, and are not a factor (on almost any front) in Japan. As part of our goal to expand our volume, Xenon absolutely must be successful in more markets, and to do that, every aspect of the plan has to address local conditions across some forty countries. This imperative requires different game content, different TV/movie content, different distribution strategies, different hardware configurations, and a different mindset across the team. If we want to be "global," we have to be "multi-local."

5. ***Think Better Together:*** As much as we all love the people in the United Nations of Xbox, with Xenon, we have to become one integrated team. The product needs to be knitted together in a more thoughtful, orchestrated way, which means the hardware and software teams need to operate as one virtual team. Our internal game developers must understand the features that differentiate the system and take advantage of them in their games; this is especially true in the depth of our support for Xbox Live. All of the development groups

should internalize the idea of a broader product so that marketing can move Xbox's positioning from "hard core gaming console" to "family entertainment system." Because we are competing with Sony, this concept of working together will reach more broadly than just the Xbox group. If the original Xbox involved separating ourselves from the broader Microsoft, Xenon requires that we work more closely with other groups to utilize the full range of Microsoft products and services.

PRIORITIES

The team has generally struggled making choices between different strategic opportunities, so we've chosen to highlight the key imperatives that must be completed successfully for Xenon to become a leadership product.

1. *Exclusive Entertainment Content and Services:* This is the highest priority because it is the lifeblood of the Xbox business. We must build a plan that utilizes Microsoft-owned franchises like Halo, some targeted games published by others like Call of Duty, and our Xbox Live services, all of which contribute to ensuring that Xenon is the best interactive entertainment platform. Our content plan must describe how we are going to utilize our key game franchises (timing, product concept, etc.), what requirements the Microsoft studios have to execute the plan, and how the platform, content, and services teams are going to work together to achieve this result. We have to do this for all of the major world markets and especially for Japan. For those titles that are going to be on both Xenon and PS3, we need to provide the right tools and ecosystem dynamics that maximize the likelihood that these titles ship at the same time on both consoles. In the ideal scenario, these titles would start as Xenon titles and migrate later to PS3.

2. *Customer Value and Differentiation:* Sony is an entrenched, established leader with 60 to 70 percent share of current generation console sales around the world. While we should be proud of our 20 to 25 percent share in North America and Europe, we have a long way to go to reach our installed base goals. Ensuring that Xenon is a clearly differentiated product that provides great customer value is critical to this effort. Differentiation starts with a clear definition of our target audience, their needs, and the experiences that excite them. Differentiation without this first step runs the risk of just "being different." Ultimately, we need value propositions that clearly state why Xenon is more valuable for each of the following target audiences: consumers, publishers, game developers, retailers, suppliers, and our internal Microsoft partners. Put differently, it is critical that we shift our value proposition away from "speeds-and-feeds performance" and focus on customer experiences (content and services). Given that we are competing with Sony,

it is especially important that we do a great job evolving and developing the Xbox brand to have strong, positive meaning for our target audiences.

3. **Profit:** Many of the tradeoffs we need to make in building the Xenon plan revolve around how much we can/want to spend acquiring customers versus returning profit to the company. I want to be clear about how we should think about this. We need to reach our critical mass sales goal, which I will define as a worldwide market share of 40 percent. Along with achieving this objective, we will optimize all of our activities around making money for Microsoft. Our goal should be for the console hardware to break even or make a small profit over the Xenon life cycle. Across the consolidated P&L (which adds Microsoft games, games from publishers, Xbox Live, sales and marketing costs, and all of our overhead), I'm challenging the team to design a business model that makes [redacted] in profit during the Xenon cycle. Profits on game content, both from Microsoft and from fees paid to us by other publishers, will make up the majority of this return. This will be supplemented by profit on peripheral products like game controllers, which were unprofitable on Xbox 1. Finally, Xbox Live must be an important source of profits targeting a [redacted] percent subscription attach rate to each console sold and [redacted] percent of the profit target. Making all of this happen will require significant changes and process improvements across all aspects of our business practices. As one example, we should design a product and business model that can last eight to ten years rather than the four- to five-year Xbox 1 life cycle.

4. **Time to Market:** We have been saying externally and internally that we would ship Xenon whenever Sony ships PS3, but we need to change this timing/approach for the internal team. If we want to gain share on Sony, we have to ship the base Xenon product by the Fall/Holiday of 2005 in all major regions (North America, Europe, Japan), and we have to make this a mandatory for the team. From a competitive perspective, we must be ready to launch at the same time they do, assuming they are on a Holiday 2005 plan. If they believe we are going in Holiday 2005, they won't be willing to risk waiting. In any event, we *must* have a differentiated offering regardless of timing, and we have the financial commitment to drive hard against Sony if they decide to wait. In terms of territory and feature tradeoffs, there is no requirement to ship in every market on the exact same day. In fact, the plan of record should reflect a staggered launch beginning in North America, moving to Europe, and finishing in Japan (where "holiday" happens later). This maximizes our ability to generate momentum through early success in our stronger markets and to build on that success in Japan. At this stage of the project, it is difficult to speculate which features we would cut or delay to hit this date, but suffice

it to say that this date is a major requirement, and we will consider feature cuts before we slip the console date.

5. ***The Fifteen-Month Campaign:*** One lesson we've learned from Xbox 1 is that "the launch" is only the first step to establishing success. With hardware supply constraints and an enthusiast audience, the laws of supply and demand encourage early positive results. But sustaining a strong start all the way through the second holiday is very challenging: the audience broadens, consoles from all competitors are in good supply, pricing and other promotional efforts play a stronger role, and content breadth and depth become even more important. Therefore, to win with Xenon, we need an integrated plan that is established well in advance to run a fifteen-month campaign which drives success from fall 2005 thru December 2006. Creating this "wave effect" means developing conscious strategies for our content and services roadmaps (down to the geography/studio/franchise/brand level) to maximize console sales. It also implies strong integration in our plans for cost reductions (which increase pricing flexibility), marketing, and sales efforts to drive share effectively. All of this is especially important if Sony decides to wait until fall 2006 to ship PS3. In that case, we will need to execute very, very well to combat their pre-launch activities.

APPENDIX B

THE AMERICAN THREE-PAGER

Author's Note: *Xbox Revisited* began as an audacious, personal quest to write a 3P Framework for the United States. Unfortunately, given the scope and scale of the issues, my first effort was more than twelve pages long and included meaningful sections on implementation tactics. Realizing that I had fallen in to a common strategy development trap, I stepped back from that document and re-crafted my approach to the problem. The American three-pager that follows is pulled directly from the text of *Xbox Revisited* but combined in one place to demonstrate how even a nation's challenges can be approached in a common-sense fashion. Because the purpose statement is drawn from the US Constitution, it is atypical for the types of statements you would craft for a 3P Framework. Fortunately, I suspect the framers had different issues on their minds at the time. Not everyone, of course, will agree with all or even most of the document, so each principle and priority deserves debate, review, and refinement. If the 3P Framework forces that discussion, it will have achieved its purpose.

A CONSTITUTIONAL PURPOSE
The framers of the United States Constitution were quite clear and specific in their mandate for a new form of government, uniquely shaped by our formative experiences:

> *We the People of the United States, in Order to form a more perfect*
> *Union, establish Justice, insure domestic Tranquility, provide for*
> *the common defence, promote the general Welfare, and secure the*
> *Blessings of Liberty to ourselves and our Posterity, do ordain and*
> *establish this Constitution for the United States of America.*

PRINCIPLES TO GUIDE US

To implement this mandate and faithfully reflect it in our actions, we must first establish a core set of principles on which we will base our action plan:

1. ***Creating Opportunity:*** The government must play a strong role in making the United States the "land of opportunity," and that prospect must be available to everyone. Part of creating this environment is building, maintaining, and upgrading the physical and intellectual infrastructure required in a modern society. Beyond that, our civil rights history has largely, and correctly, been focused on creating opportunity for disadvantaged or discriminated groups. Opening the right to vote to all citizens, the long belated Civil Rights Movement in the 1960s and Title IX are good examples of pursuing equal opportunity, and even in these areas there is much more to be done. Although I'm not sure the original framers of the Constitution had this in mind, providing a safety net that supports those most in need is an essential element to leading a modern society. This approach generates an ongoing tension between creating opportunity and trying to ensure equality of outcomes. The government cannot afford to manage, ensure, or orchestrate outcomes effectively, nor should it try. Actual outcomes are a function of individual skill/effort, social and market forces, and the laws of chance and providence. Establishing the boundary between opportunity and outcomes is a difficult balancing act, but one that must be achieved.

2. ***Living within Our Means:*** The government should never run just like a business, but responsible government requires a recognition that revenue and expenses are related and financial results must remain within certain boundaries. The government has to live within its means with revenues and expenses growing or shrinking in a synchronous way. Of course, the government can and should borrow to finance some spending activities. In particular, in times of crisis, debt provides real, economic leverage and is actually valuable for the country. But just as with personal or business affairs, this borrowing must fit within certain limits. At the state and local levels, real constraints exist, both constitutionally and practically, that force and maintain this equilibrium. For the federal budget, however, few structured safeguards exist, so it's imperative to establish and follow a self-imposed, rational business model that supports today's needs but also preserves economic strength for future generations.

3. ***Investing for the Future:*** If the goal is to "insure domestic Tranquility" and provide for "our Posterity," the planning-time horizon must shift significantly. For far too long, the US economy has expanded based on an underlying premise of cheap credit, high consumption, and government policies that have supported and accelerated this approach. Even though this leads to

periods of episodic growth, it also sets the stage for the inevitable collapse, the latest of which deeply wounded and divided the country. Going forward, investment, innovation, and production must be engines of growth rather than counting on short-term fixes that amount to nothing more than Band Aids. Leaders and voters need to have the patience and foresight to invest in programs and policies for the long term and give them enough time to germinate and grow.

4. ***Balancing Rights and Responsibilities:*** To a remarkable level, the founding fathers focused on establishing the rights of individuals and delineating between the rights and responsibilities of the states and the federal government. In addition to the core of the Constitution, the Bill of Rights and several other amendments make clear that the social contract with all levels of government is based on the premise that citizens come first. The government certainly must pass laws that regulate behavior, build underlying infrastructure, and arbitrate between groups and individuals. But these roles should be reserved for as few things as necessary to "promote the general Welfare." The corollary to this principle is that there should be as little government as is required to fulfill our purpose and that as many issues as possible should be left to individual states or private citizens to arbitrate as befits their local circumstances. Unfortunately, we have allowed federal and state governments to infringe on this principle too frequently.

5. ***Fostering the Melting Pot:*** The United States has an incredible history of welcoming and integrating new citizens, new cultures, and new philosophies into the "American Way." Wave after wave of immigrants, beginning with the Jamestown colony and the Pilgrims right through to the current Hispanic, Asian, and Eastern European migrations, have come to our country looking for a new start. African Americans arrived against their will and have faced tremendous discrimination, but they have persevered nonetheless. Although these cultural combinations often involve real tension and acrimony, we somehow manage to find our way to a broader consensus. Each new group enriches our culture, our intellectual capability, and our human resource in different ways, and that is a tremendous source of strength. While not easy, continuing to welcome newcomers in spite of real security issues and imagined insecurities is important to long-term growth and prosperity.

PRIORITIES BRING FOCUS

Given the depth and breadth of the challenges we face, there are many issues and initiatives we could pursue. The five priorities proposed below are based on the purpose and principles already articulated and reflect in particular the long-term needs of our country.

1. ***Economic Common Sense:*** At the core of the debate over priorities lies the fundamental dysfunction in the country's business model. Many of the nation's challenges begin and end with questions about economic status; poor education, crime, obesity, addictions, government dependence, and family dysfunction all are positively correlated with poverty. The simple act of getting and holding a job that pays a living wage has a tremendous impact on individuals' lives and on the economy collectively, and employment is the most powerful tool to reduce the wealth gap that is driving a schism in our social framework. Consequently, improving our employment environment is an essential element in restructuring our economy.

   In fiscal terms, while spending levels have continued to grow, both in absolute terms and relative to the size of the economy, there has been a corresponding set of pressures to limit tax increases; provide tax incentives for various programs; and support certain special interest groups, industries, and classes of individuals. As any economist, business leader, or head of household will tell you, continually increasing expenses and constraining revenue is a recipe for disaster. The US economy can certainly support more debt than most, so this is not a proposal for a balanced budget. Instead, it is focused on bringing balance to the budget. On current course and speed, according to one likely scenario from the Congressional Budget Office, entitlement expenses and interest on the national debt will consume 100 percent of government revenues by 2025. Even if this is off by five years one way or the other, this is a serious problem.

   The solution involves, at the same time, complexity and common sense and definitely requires some courage. We must be willing to rethink defense, Medicare/Medicaid, Social Security, and other entitlement programs that account for roughly 75 percent of today's federal budget. At the same time, we must recognize that tax revenue (and tax rates for some) must increase. In short, the government must develop a more balanced, sensible economic model for operations. The National Commission on Fiscal Responsibility and Reform (otherwise known as the Simpson-Bowles Commission) summarizes it this way: "After all the talk about debt and deficits, it is long past time for America's leaders to put up or shut up. The era of debt denial is over, and there can be no turning back."

2. ***Education Transformation:*** A Chinese proverb wisely says, "When planning for a year, plant corn. When planning for a decade, plant trees. When planning for life, train and educate people." If the goal is to change the course of the country's development, America must lead the world in educating young people. And yet we have gone from a nation with one of the best overall education systems to one that struggles with the basics of reading, writing, mathematics, and science. We are now ranked twenty-seventh in math scores

and twenty-second in science, according to OECD data. Twenty-five percent of high school age students will not graduate, and the social and economic costs and implications of that failure are staggering. We are raising a lost generation of children. As Frederick Douglas said, "It is easier to build strong children than to repair broken men."

Urgent reform is required to reinvent our approach to education, and that reform has to start by measuring and rewarding quality teaching and removing those who are not good at their craft. Taken as a whole, students don't spend enough time on the core academic subjects that matter and lose ground over an overly long summer break. Students must be reached at the critical pivot points in their education, in particular in early learning and in sixth to eighth grades. Finally, post-secondary training is often a better path for many young adults than an expensive, four-year institution. Reshaping the education system is a long-term infrastructure project that will require patience and consistency to show progress. It also will require collaborative work between school administrations, teachers/unions, community service organizations, and parents. Enough money is already allocated if it is spent wisely and focused on the areas that matter most.

3. **Environment and Energy Investment:** This discussion begins at first principles: mankind is having a meaningful and largely negative impact on the Earth's environment with carbon emissions and the subsequent warming of the planet as the most serious issue. It is time to get over the inconvenient truth and work to solve the problem. At the same time, America's lack of a sustainable, independent energy supply is a constant drain on the country and a source of many security concerns. In combination, climate deterioration and unsustainable energy policies will over time make it difficult to provide proper food and water and will negatively affect economic growth with particular impact on the poor.

Ultimately, this is where the environment and energy create a perfect storm of need: developing energy sources that are environmentally sound, domestically sourced, renewable, and economically practical must be a key objective to generate sustainable growth and broader economic prosperity. This effort requires a dramatic increase in core science and technology investments with the government tripling or quadrupling the amount of money it awards for core research—research that should be conducted in partnerships involving the public sector, universities, and private enterprises. Since this approach will take time to yield practical fruits, conservation will be an important and required part of the strategy, along with the utilization of transitional technologies like natural gas to generate interim energy solutions. In the process, the usage of coal as an important energy source must be eliminated due to its environmental side effects. When it comes to the environment and energy, everyone must ask this question: "Twenty-five years from now, will our surviving children look back and say, 'What were they thinking?'"

4. **Equal Opportunity Support:** None of these challenges is as complicated or emotional as the need to provide for those who require assistance. There absolutely is a moral imperative to understand the needs of those who are less fortunate and develop ways to help them. Chronic unemployment, homelessness, and hunger describe some of the most basic challenges to address, but there are others, such as mental health, addictions, abuse, and parentless children. These problems must be attacked in a manner that is fiscally responsible and leads to an improved circumstance for those receiving aid, so that over time, they can become self-sufficient.

Programs must change from "entitlements" (and the social attitudes that go with that word) to enrichment programs that enable people to scale up. While the government certainly must play a significant role in this process, current state and federal programs are plagued by inefficiencies, duplicative design, and generally poor outcome measurement. Healthy partnerships are required among government, the private sector, and nonprofits to build a durable and scalable safety net that truly provides equal opportunities to as many citizens as possible. To create this system, every program must have a set of criteria and metrics that are measured and tracked to make sure money is being spent effectively. This outcomes-based approach will enable the removal of programs that are not performing and offer enhancements to those that produce results. In the end, providing everyone with an opportunity for success boils down to a human choice. Again, we must ask ourselves the basic question: "If I were in their shoes, how would I want to be treated?"

5. **Global Engagement:** Whether we like it or not, the world is a scary place, and one of the federal government's primary roles is defense. While I am not a fan of engaging in needless conflicts, we have to invest both militarily and diplomatically in protecting our interests—and those interests absolutely involve activities in other countries. The ongoing conflicts in the Middle East, the latest twist in our relationship with Russia, the crazy leadership in countries like North Korea, and the risks associated with terrorism and nuclear proliferation are all real threats to the American people.

Protecting our citizens successfully requires an effective military capability, world-class intelligence gathering, and constructive diplomatic skills. The goal is not to be the world's policeman, leading arms dealer, or global bully—the time for those attitudes has long passed. Instead, we should focus our energies on identifying threats to American security, building appropriate partnerships that advance our regional interests and supporting humanitarian efforts when appropriate.

International affairs is about much more than just providing protection—in fact, it includes promoting global trade, opening new markets, and supporting third-world development, all of which are essential to economic growth. In many respects, our economic strength and business success is both dependent on foreign policy success and one of our best and most important foreign policy tools. Developing and supporting prosperity, both at home and abroad, is a powerful way to win friends and create influence beyond our borders. And in deference to our economic common-sense priority, all of this can be accomplished for significantly less money than we are spending in this area today.

ABOUT THE AUTHOR

Robbie Bach joined Microsoft in 1988 and over the next twenty-two years worked in various marketing, general management, and business leadership roles, including working on the successful launch and expansion of Microsoft Office. As Chief Xbox Officer, he led the creation and development of the Xbox business, including the launch of the Xbox and the highly popular successor product, Xbox 360. He retired from Microsoft in 2010 as the president of the Entertainment and Devices Division.

In his new role as civic engineer, Robbie currently serves on the national board of governors for the Boys and Girls Clubs of America and was the chairman of the board from 2009-10. He is also a board member of the United States Olympic Committee, Sonos Inc., Brooks Running Company, the Space Needle Inc., and local chapters of Boys and Girls Clubs and Year Up. Robbie is a regular guest lecturer at universities across the country and frequently writes on business and civic issues. All profits from his writing and speaking activities are donated to charity. (See www.RobbieBach.com for more information.)

Robbie received an MBA from Stanford University and his bachelor's degree in economics from the University of North Carolina, where he was a Morehead Scholar and named a first team Academic All-American on the Tar Heel's tennis team.

He currently resides in Medina, Washington with his wife, Pauline, and their three children.